What Happens When
WOMEN
Wake Up?

PATRICIA FERO

ISBN 978-0-9767932-0-2

Patricia Fero
3830 Packard St, Ste 250
Ann Arbor, MI 48108
(734) 973-7026
Cell: (734) 717-8384
e-mail: pat_fero@yahoo.com

When sleeping women wake, mountains move.
—Chinese proverb

This book is dedicated to author and spiritual leader Marianne Williamson, whose work has inspired me. She is an awake woman who walks ahead and shows us the way.

CONTENTS

Acknowledgments

Writing this book has been a labor of love. The gifts I received in acquainting and then immersing myself in the Sacred Feminine are immeasurable. The connections I made enriched and deepened me. Living in the spirit of this creation has been an awakening process for me.

My first thank you goes to this book for asking me to write it. I've known from the beginning it was my "Divine Assignment." What I didn't know was the wealth it offered me. For this, I am powerfully grateful.

I began this book on Christmas Eve 2006 when the energy burst forth like a Fourth of July fireworks display. I was finally beginning to emerge from one of the most painful periods of my life when I called Lynn from the Whole Foods cafeteria and said, "I'm beginning writing *What Happens When Women Wake Up?* today."

Lynn, your support, encouragement, and guidance shifted into high gear that morning and continued every morning for the next two years. Your guidance and insights are intrinsically woven throughout the entire process. The Divine orchestration of our meeting set the stage for this synergy.

It seems so long ago that Ann mentored me, and we met every Friday morning at Expresso Royale. Ann, your expertise, encouragement, and belief in my capabilities changed me in the most remarkable way. Your brilliant scripting of questions for the interviews sparked compelling responses as the women told their stories of waking up. As you know, your inspired direction kept the book alive whenever it seemed to be failing. Without your skilled interventions I'm not sure I would have completed my assignment.

Next comes, Nene, my soul sister in Spirit. You began communicating with me three days after your beautiful spirit left your painful body. We both know you are my co-author. The next book is for you, Nene.

The essence of the 24 women who agreed to share their stories are woven throughout the book. We felt the momentum build as we moved through the beautifully crafted interview questions until each of you ended with your unique understanding of the role of the collective feminine in planetary awakening. Each of these "diamonds" of insight is polished up and included in the last part of the book titled Call to Action: Women Waking the World.

Nina Diamond, my editor continues to be an expert at *Mining for Diamonds*. You were so skillful in uncovering the diamonds in my writings and polishing them up to create a beautiful setting for each.

Jan, my life coach, and now cherished friend cheered, inspired, and encouraged me beyond limits. Your driving from Toronto to Ann Arbor to spend an entire marathon weekend working with me when I was floundering exemplifies your generous spirit. The relationship that we developed as you coached me through all the obstacles is a priceless treasure.

The support and gifts I've been given could fill another book. A powerful opening occurred when I made my first phone call to Marilyn Nyborg. Thank you Marilyn, for the energetic container you seeded with *Gather the Women, Global Matrix*; and *Women Waking the World*. Being aligned with your visionary energy has brought me to places I didn't know existed.

I am so grateful, Sandy, for your collaboration on the Essence Statements and generosity with your amazing guidance. Thanks also to Lani for your generous editing and moral support; Jonathon for being my spiritual director; Julie for your support and encouragement. Gratitude to you Mike for being who you are. The depth of our 30 year friendship, and the power of our "Ferocious meetings" have mobilized me in ways you understand better than anyone.

The magic of the creation of the book was supported by you Kristin for seeing that I was being "buoyed up on a Golden Raft"; Jacque for your support and joyful efforts; Debbie for being there as a cheerleader throughout the process, and your guidance about "the quilt"; Gretchen, our friendship continues to grow stronger since we met in 1983. I value you so much. Vikki, our goddess retreat, fueled the process as did your inspired creation of an altar which provided focus and spiritual nourishment. Thanks for being my soul sister. Patricia, your kindness, patience, and skill in your manuscript typing helped so much in the final phases. Leah, your transposing all those interviews was a crucial piece of the process. I am so grateful, Kathy, for your ongoing support then and now. Lastly Diana, thank you for your friendship and brilliant idea that inspired the final arrangement of the quilt pieces.

Foreword: Dawn

Morning has broken, like the first morning.
—Cat Stevens

Imagine a woman who descends into the richness of her own life. A woman who awakens to her truth and wisdom, her gifts and capacities. A woman who grows in knowledge and love of herself. Who remains loyal to herself, regardless.

Imagine a woman who gathers the gifts of her awakening…a freed imagination, a courageous rebellion, the acceptance of her body, the accumulation of her years, the expression of her wholeness and wisdom. A woman who offers these sacred gifts to our vulnerable world—out of balance, estranged from wisdom, and addicted to power.

Imagine a circle of awakened women, who love themselves. Women who reorder the world by giving birth to images of inclusion, poems of truth, rituals of healing, experiences of transformation, relationships of equality, strategies of peace, institutions of justice, and households of compassion. Women, full of themselves for the sake of their children and their children's children, for the sake of their beloved planet.

Imagine sitting in the circle of women, past, present, and future, as you read the insights and stories gathered by Patricia Fero, inspired by the question *What Happens When Women*

Wake Up? The storytellers' voices are strong *and* tender, inviting us to awaken from our sleep, to rise out of our stupor, to return home after the long exile.

One by one they speak the truth of a woman's life told with their hearts, minds, and bodies. They gather our brokenness into their words. As we listen, an impulse toward wholeness awakens within us and we become again, as we once were, whole. We rise from our slumber, splash cold water on our faces, welcome the new day, and in the company of women from every age, we reorder the world with clarity, courage, and strength. And so it is!

Patricia Lynn Reilly
Author of *Imagine a Woman in Love with Herself*

Author's Note

When I began writing *When Women Wake Up*, I ran into an old mentor and we discussed the question that became the title of the book, "What Happens When Women Wake Up?"

She suddenly responded, "We stand up and form a matrix of Love and Light that heals the planet." These words came out because she is awakening. She has access to her Core Essence Self and allows herself to speak from this part of herself.

As I moved further along in my writing process, I discovered Marilyn Nyborg and Gather the Women, which began building a global matrix in 2003 and now includes thousands of women worldwide. Gather the Women is an energetic container that supports the awakening of the collective feminine as it is emerging on the planet. It is a significant catalyst for the planetary awakening we are now in the midst of, for the awakening of women everywhere.

Marilyn Nyborg created the DVD *Seeding the Circles*, a compilation of short talks by Barbara Marx Hubbard, Jean Shinoda Bolen, and Jean Houston, the three women Marilyn humorously refers to as "the wholly trinity" because each of these amazing pioneers lead the way. In the DVD they speak about the emerging feminine energies and the catalytic role these energies play in the planet's awakening we are beginning to experience.

Eckhert Tolle, in his book *The New Earth*, calls this awakening "the flowering of a new consciousness."

As you read you will see what happens when women are asleep and what happens when they wake up. You will learn how connecting with the Core Essence Self is the key to staying awake. Throughout the book you will meet 11 remarkable women who have awakened and who show us the way. The final section is a call to action that propels women to wake up the world and save it.

My hope and intention is that this book will play a part in your awakening, as well as the emerging energies that are awakening the planet.

What is Waking Up?

Who looks outside dreams, and who looks inside wakes.
—C. C. Jung

Waking up is connecting to the essence of who you are.

The dictionary definition of essence is: "that which makes a thing what it is; true inward nature."

The socialization process, especially for girls and women in a patriarchal culture, requires consistent movement *away* from that essence. This moving away takes the form of adapting, pleasing, and relinquishing power.

Waking up is a return to the Self, a discovery, connection, and nourishing of the Core Essence Self that is the seed of divinity within each of us.

Waking up is a process, not a single event, although many women report a "wake-up call" that starts them on this path of Self awareness that continues throughout their lives. The cumulative effect of this connection to Self creates the awareness that you are awake, and the ultimate state of being awake is enlightenment.

In his landmark book, *Many Lives, Many Masters*, Brian Weiss compares the Core Essence Self to a large multifaceted diamond within each of us. While everyone has the diamond within, each of us has varying levels of debris on the diamond's facets. This debris is the result of the socialization process, the attachment to ego, and unhealed wounds. The cleaning off of the diamond's facets is the waking up process—removing what is not of the Core Essence Self.

The completely polished, residue-free diamond would be enlightenment or being fully awake.

The *process* of waking up leads to the *experience* of being awake.

Awakening is a process, but also a way of *being* in the world.

The most famous image of the metaphor for sleeping and awakening is the fairy tale character Sleeping Beauty, who embodies the key energies of being spiritually asleep: she's passive, she's waiting, she demonstrates little awareness of her own power within, and she is dependent on someone (the prince) and something (the kiss) to wake her up so she can take her place in the world.

This is the archetype of a woman asleep, and the effect of a patriarchal culture.

The awake woman, on the other hand, is standing in her *own* power, connected to the awareness of Self, and radiating the energy of her power. With her feet planted firmly on Mother Earth and her arms raised to Father Sky, she is the healthy, natural balance of feminine and masculine energies. She has power in the world, and she experiences herself in communion with the Divine as the source of power.

Waking Up is an Inside Job

Dig within. Within is the spring well of good, and
it is always ready to bubble up if you just dig.
—Marcus Aurelius

The path to awakening and enlightenment is always an individual one.

As a psychotherapist working primarily with women, I see co-dependency—a relinquishment of one's own power for the sake of a relationship—as the primary vehicle for women remaining asleep. I educate consistently about the distinction between being *self-referenced* as opposed to *other-referenced.*

With *self-referral,* you look to the Self for information and power. With *other-referral,* you look outside yourself for information and power.

Are the answers and the power within *you,* or do you look to *others* for them? Do you have your *own* sense of Self, identity, opinions, and desires, or do you believe you don't have a right to those, and simply acquiesce to the power of *other* people? Do you have the faith in *yourself* and the courage to be yourself or do you need another's approval to be yourself or the version of your Self that you believe you have to be, in order to not make waves or to preserve another person's power?

The waking up process is an evolution out of the patriarchal hierarchical paradigm of externalized power to the gradual acceptance of internalized power, and ultimately, the divine power within as the origin from which we experience and express who we are in the world.

Waking Up is an Act of Power

> Ultimately…it's not the stories that determine our
> choices, but the stories that we continue to choose.
> —Sylvia Boorstein

Often, a crisis or wake-up call prompts a woman to change her trajectory and simultaneously shift her perception of herself from other-referral to self-referral. The stories with women who show us the way describe such wake-up calls. From there, our work and our choices continue until we experience the cumulative effect of progressively more choices that lie in favor of self-referral and the Self.

The hold of the "outer" on a woman's identity and choices continues to diminish until ultimately the woman awake sees herself as the author and authority of her own life.

When women wake up, they:

- reclaim their power because being asleep is powerlessness;
- each become the central figure in their own life;
- quit waiting for someone else to take care of them;
- create a "no bullshit zone," ending psychological and physical violence;

- form a matrix of love and light by helping each other, connecting with others, operating under the laws of attraction, and role modeling;

- heal the planet and raise its vibrations, honor and invite back Divine feminine energy, and take their rightful place in the "Cosmic Choir" and ground this to earthly experience.

You will learn about all of these elements of the woman awake throughout this book, and meet 11 women who have awakened, embody these elements, and can show us all the way.

Becoming the Central Figure in Your Own Life

> You yourself, as much as anybody in the entire
> universe, deserve your love and affection.
> —Buddha

When women wake up, they become the central figure in their own lives. This concept elicits so much resistance because women have been so strongly programmed to play supportive roles.

The mother role centers around meeting the needs of her children. The wife role centers around supporting her husband in his endeavors in the world as well as taking care of his needs at home, often as if he were a child. The homemaker role centers around tending to the needs and responsibilities of the house and everyone else in it. The professional roles available to women have been traditionally restricted to supportive ones: nurse, teacher or social worker. Only in the last three decades have wider professional roles been consistently open to women.

With married women and single mothers playing so many supporting and professional roles simultaneously, how and where in the world do women find the time, energy, and permission to become the central figure in their own lives? And isn't that selfish?

This is the most common question asked when women are introduced to the concept of and necessity for self-care. In fact, most women are confused by the idea that they even *have* a Self (or have the *right* to have a Self), and that it requires and deserves attention. They have been programmed to believe that the notion is selfish. Nothing could be further from the truth. Awareness of, connection to, respect for, and care of the Self is *every* human being's divine right, whether that human being is male or female, child or adult. Without healthy attention to Self, ironically, we can't give healthy energy to others, and the imbalance can be quite self-destructive.

Hilary Hart quotes Lynn Barron in *The Unknown She,* "One of the greatest obstacles for women is to understand that all is within." She continues, "Because women are so relational, we want to be in relationship to something outside ourselves for the qualities and elements we need." She wisely points out that, "There can be so many obstacles for women; just the conditioned roles in our relationships; just the idea that we nurture and care. If you are the type of person who will nurture and care for every individual who comes into your experience, then you are in big trouble because you will never find the time or inner dimension necessary to develop that quiet contemplative place within yourself that will allow the grace to come." Lynn concludes that "one of the hardest things to accept is that you have to learn to be completely alone. It's the idea of living completely within yourself."

This is a foreign and frightening concept for most women, but it's a concept we must embrace if we are to become the central figure in our own lives. When we become the central figure in our own lives, we then connect with and nurture others from a place of awakened wholeness and self-referral.

Recently, a young mother boasted to me that she only slept

for three or four hours a night because she was always doing things for other people. She even said that she was never home unless her children were home from school because she can't stand being alone. This woman is married to a man who works 12 hours a day at a highly stressful job. She chooses not to work and add to the family's financial support because she says, "She's always only wanted to be a wife and mother." Her children are in school, and she busies herself with trivia because she has no interests of her own and stubbornly refuses to connect with herself internally. Her husband is resentful, and she's dependent and manipulative. This is an example of a woman living at the effect of a patriarchal culture, a woman asleep.

As we present these outdated, unhealthy, uninspiring examples of womanhood to our daughters, we lose even more precious time in contributing to the improvement of the human experience on the planet. When we act as the central figure in our own life, we offer an awakened, healthy, inspiring example to others who then can grow to contribute significantly because they've *seen* women walking this path.

Kristin

Kristin's awakening came when she
stopped being afraid to know herself. She
expressed herself, and let her spirit fly.

Kristin

Power is the ability not to have to please.
—Elizabeth Janeway

When I was asleep I was looking to external sources to know who I was. It was just like being a child looking at your parent to know who you are. That extended into my marriage at 19, and I continued that. I'd look to my husband to know who I was. It was confusing because I didn't always feel that what was being told to me was true, but I was afraid. So I suppressed that feeling and tried my best to be what I was *told* to be.

Every once in a while, the feeling would push out and it came out as depression and as an eating disorder. I was pretty good at suppressing the feelings. I really had no awareness. I just knew that I had strange reactions sometimes. I didn't even want to know why I had those reactions.

In my 20s, my husband and I and one of his associates were at dinner and he said that he and his wife like to go to workshops so they could learn what's under the surface, who they really are, and how to relate to each other more fully. I thought that sounded like the most frightening thing to do because I had a sense that I was a thin, brittle crust over something very scary.

I desperately hoped to be rescued. I thought of that song "Some Day My Prince Will Come," and I thought it would be just like Snow White in a coma, and that I would just be touched by magic. Or that I'd be Cinderella and I'd be discovered, that I would be lifted up out of my oppressive marriage to an authoritarian husband. Of course, I'd inadvertently asked him to be authoritarian because I was nonverbally asking him who I was. So, of course, he became increasingly even more authoritarian as time went on. But I imagined that some magical event would occur from outside.

I had always studied metaphysics, and it should have given me a broader picture, but I used it to clamp down on my feelings. I said to myself, that's a bad thought, and bad thoughts create bad reality, so I must cleanse my mind of all negative thinking. So for example, I can't think of defiance or rebellion against my authoritarian husband or against my role as a devoted mother.

I'd known about another reality since I was a teenager because I started studying metaphysics at about 11 or 12. My mother started talking about metaphysics, and I read about it when I was quite young. But, in my marriage, and in the oppression that I was experiencing, I used metaphysics to further oppress myself because of my fear. I didn't want to know anything more. *Not* to know was a survival tactic. I wanted to stay in a very traditional role because I was afraid that I couldn't survive in our society as a single woman or a single parent. I thought that I would collapse emotionally because I had no sense of believing in myself. I had felt pretty depressed as a teenager and I had a lot of conflict with my parents then, so I felt there was nowhere for me to get that support that I would've needed to strengthen myself or function well as a single person. It was a fear of abandonment. There was nobody else, there was no family, no friends that I trusted. I didn't let myself think about anything.

When I was in my early 30s, I invested even further in deliberately being unconscious and decided that I would survive even *better* than before by being more attractive, playful, and extroverted. I created an adopted persona. So, my false persona was deepened by looking more fashionable, and acting giddy and entertaining. It's very painful to look back at that because I was even more detached from my deeper Self than when I was a teenager. When I was a teenager, I was the serious, bookish one known for quiet dignity. As an adult, I even gave *that* away. I went to social events with my husband, and I just threw myself into the role of being vivacious. I did it as a safety measure because I was concerned that my husband was wandering. That was very frightening to me. I had some evidence that it was a possibility. So I thought I had to be more attractive. The blindness or darkness deepened in my 30s. I'd pull out of depression by dressing up and getting vivacious to go to a party, or if I was at home, I'd do housework or gardening until I felt some endorphins.

I was very happy with my three children at the time. But I felt suspicious and alienated from my husband and increasingly so as time went on.

I was pushed into the waking up process. If it weren't for this push, I might *still* be the obedient housewife. I was financially pushed into returning to school to finish my bachelor's degree and working to put my children through college. At the end of the 1970s there was a real high rate of inflation, and my husband was changing jobs and floundering in his confidence. The inflation was frightening for everybody.

When I left the house I discovered that everybody treated me better than he did. During 19 years of marriage I hadn't been in the outside world. I'd thought I wouldn't be able to survive outside the front door. I was quite agoraphobic at the time. I had a lot of panic attacks when I was shopping at the mall, and I was very, very stressed in any social situations.

During this crisis what kicked in was my memory of having worked at 15 when my parents went through financial difficulties. I'd promised my husband I could get a job and make the difference in getting our children through college. I went into another part of my persona. Then came this big jump in awareness that there was a Self in there besides where I'd been functioning. I saw that everybody believed in me, and I had some skills. Everywhere I turned I was able to do one thing and then the next thing. I was getting a great deal of reinforcement and respect for my abilities. People seemed to like me and enjoy me and seek me out for just plain hanging-out fun. So, school and work was intoxicating after years of the authoritarian, demeaning treatment by my husband, who did not relate to me as an equal. He acted like a teacher or parent and he felt very comfortable in that role.

I started feeling some authentic power, natural power. I was getting promotions. My husband started treating me better. When he'd go to some of my professional events, he'd say, "Well, I can see that you're well thought of by the way people are treating you." This was after quite a few years of moving ahead in my career. I was almost obsessed by my career because I realized I'd been in this deep, dark well that I was climbing out of one hand over the other, one foot over the other. I had so much reinforcement. It was so exciting that I was doing everything I could get my hands on just to experience my own abilities. These endeavors included doing volunteer work like being president of my alumni association; being on the board of governors for the alumni association and going to big retreats with people from all over the country and giving presentations.

One after the other, my children were going to college and I missed them. But I felt that what I was doing made me a better parent and a better support for them. As a fully-developed professional person, I was enjoying them more. So, that was a phase of about 10 years. First almost 20 years of being at home in the darkness, then 10 years of an accelerated self-discovery in the professional arena. I had lost my faith in metaphysics at that time because I felt that it added to my oppression. I thought, I've got energy, drive, intellect, I'm just gonna do whatever I can on a very human plane to get my kids through college and be a good example of making something of myself.

Then I had another awakening. It was another very profound shake up, and it opened up my perspective of what I was doing to myself. I was becoming the career robot. I saw that I'd really sacrificed my physical and emotional well-being for this experience of getting ahead, almost with a vengeance.

My husband had put me down, and I was going to show him that I could be on top. But, I'd sacrificed a lot for that fearful pursuit of my career. I suddenly saw it on a visit with some friends. I was treated with sweetness by them and had five days of riding horseback in the mountains, and I began to feel the more sensual Self that I really needed to thaw out. I started to feel the thaw of the rigid way I'd held myself.

After five days on their farm herding cattle, riding horseback in the mountains, having wonderful dinner parties, and just laughing and being a silly human being instead of the career robot, I headed back home and I cried most of the nine-hour drive because I realized I couldn't go back to that frozen, rigid life. I'd been working 70 hours a week. I finished my master's degree and an internship at the same time, I was working full-time, and I was also traveling for my job. I knew I couldn't go back to that life.

So, I came home and changed everything. I got some confidence from having enjoyed finishing my Master's degree, and I thought, I did *that*, I can do these *other* things, too, I could ask for a divorce, or at least ask for a better relationship. It turned out that my husband was thinking about divorce, too, so it was hard to resist the divorce. And hard to resist just finding a simple place to live and not being in the big house I'd raised my children in. I quit my job at the university and I became a psychotherapist.

I started to know that I could do whatever I wanted to do and needed to do. I made a life with friends and had some adventures, and got to know my children without the presence of their father, which was very liberating. It was nice to get to know them as people, instead of playing the role of mother and disgruntled partner of their father.

It was difficult, but I made it. I began to have faith in the human Self at a deeper level. After that decade of being the career person, I had another decade of learning that I was a human being, too, and that I'd be all right in the world. I had nothing to fear making a life.

I'm 65 now. I had a crisis that really brought me to my knees at about 59, and it catapulted me onto the spiritual path because I'd believed in psychology as my religion. But it was failing me, and I was beginning to get glimpses of something in my patients—I was learning about the human spirit. I couldn't deny that there was something way beyond any of the psychology that I had learned from brilliant professors. In my postgraduate fellowship in classical analysis, nothing touched this mystery that I was experiencing in my work. Over this decade as a psychotherapist, I'd really let go of the disciplined analytic role that

I'd been trained in, and I was more eclectic, but I still was very aware of this mystery.

I guess I was ready to be shaken into my own discovery of the inner spirituality that I'd denied in myself since I'd learned about metaphysics as an 11-year-old.

I had a nervous breakdown and couldn't leave my house and had to take medication to prevent continual panic. Two trusted friends and my children gathered around me and stayed with me for a week until my psychotherapy work pulled me out of it. I had EMDR treatments for dissociate tendencies because my false persona that I'd so carefully constructed had failed me. It was ripe for failing because it left me with nothing else. I was like a baby without the false persona.

I started feeling stronger and I was able to integrate other parts of myself that I had denied, that I had discredited, that I thought were useless. I embraced these hidden and neglected parts of myself and found that there was a wholeness that I could rely on that included a reverence for life and the Divine. I wanted to know more. So I started searching to learn more about this deeper inner Self that was associated with the Divine.

After a few months, I started to feel better and began to go to all kinds of workshops. Then I went to an Ayurvedic preventative workshop. That started my association with an Ayurvedic physician who guided me in detoxifying my physiology and eating the correct diet and using the right herbs for balancing my energy. I was invited to participate in a healing session with Ayurvedic technicians who were trained in India. I wanted to have a healing from them for anxiety. I did, and I've never had a panic attack again.

I thought, there is something here that's very powerful and mysterious. I went to some more healings for depression and arthritis through the next year and finally decided to learn transcendental meditation because I thought it would give me this healing energy in my own life every day.

I took the training for transcendental meditation, and I had my most profound experience of having hope that I could have a peaceful and happy life. I felt myself become grounded for the first time ever in my life. I went home and I found I could do it on my own. From then on, my meditation has given me my lifeline to being able to be on this planet and have a good experience and feel connected to the spiritual aspect of myself.

I'm experiencing moments of real pleasure, bliss, and happiness, and a close connection with my children and their spouses. I'm just recently experiencing life in an entirely different way than I had in my 20s, which was my first decade of my marriage; or my 30s, which was when I acted out the geisha role out of desperation to keep my marriage; or my 40s, which was when I was the career robot; or my 50s, which was when I became a psychotherapist trying to function more as a whole human being. Now, I'm in my 60s, so this seems to be the decade of discovering the feeling of oneness.

Now, when I do my work as a psychotherapist, when I interact with my family, and when I'm with my friends, I feel that the deeper part of the Self that's connected to the Divine that has the potential to experience the oneness.

I feel a source of energy that's very stable, and a source of ideas that's very clear. I feel like I have something buoying me up and carrying me through everyday life that makes it easier to function. I have very steady physical energy and steady moods. I don't get tired and grouchy. My thinking feels very clear. Anything that comes up I just know that there's a way through it and I'll handle it. I just have to wait and listen. I know that whatever

I need to do will become very clear to me. That hasn't failed me. That sense of the natural harmony of the universe has been with me and hasn't failed.

I haven't pursued things that didn't seem right. Things that seemed natural and easy have just come up that have enhanced my life. Every day seems like a natural expression of the universe flowing in an intelligent way. I ride with it and listen. I watch for what seems to be the right thing. So, it's fun.

1) What parts of Kristin's story remind you of yourself?

2) Kristin created several adopted personas to support her sleep state. In what ways do you create a social mask, false persona?

3) With what people do you feel more authentic power more connected to yourself?

4) Kristin was not rescued by Prince Charming but saved herself. How are you rescuing yourself?

5) How do you nourish your relationship with yourself? How did Kristin support her awakening process? How could you do this for yourself?

No Longer Waiting

The doors we open and close each day decide the lives we live.
—Flora Whittemore

One of the crucial things that happens when women wake up is that they stop waiting for someone else to take care of them and take care of whatever needs doing, including saving the planet.

Women have been immersed in the energy of waiting. With this waiting energy dominating their lives, immeasurable amounts of initiative have lain dormant.

Stereotypically, men have been the carriers of initiative, the ones who take action. By this same model, women carry the feelings and the nurturing, but wait for the men to take action. Women who *do* take action, have been criticized, sneered at suspiciously, labeled "bitches," and deemed somehow less feminine. Until the latter part of the 20th century in Western cultures, plenty of laws and social regulations have reined women in, and they continue to do so—often with violent and fatal consequences—in many countries around the world. Clearly, this model has never worked well, and doesn't now.

The actions taken by an unbalanced patriarchal worldwide culture have brought us abuses of personal and public power, and brought us to the brink of annihilation. Does continuing to wait for the men to take care of us (while we hope not to be insulted, reined in, and abused in the process) and take care of the planet seem the best plan of action?

Observations of young girls demonstrate that at the age girls start becoming interested in boys, the girls' personal initiative decreases and the game of focusing on appearance and waiting for the boy to take the initiative begins.

Girls and women are consistently told that boys don't like it when girls take the initiative (in romance, or anything else), and that boys are programmed to, and like to, take the initiative, be in charge, and, in the case of romance, chase after *you*.

So many life experiences are lost when a woman believes that she has to wait for the right man to come along before her life can really begin; before she can create a home; before she can create a family. Home and family can be very broadly defined and shouldn't insulate women from the rest of the world as virtual prisoners, waiting and waiting.

As a therapist, I see so often that waiting for the right man is the *only* goal of women, both young and older. Who these women are and their full potential in the world lies unexplored. Waiting for him, and then waiting for the family, and then even waiting for the grandchildren, is a very narrow focus in a very big world.

The energy of waiting at this crucial time in the world is not only terribly outdated, but irresponsible and destructive. An awake woman does not wait for someone else to take care of her or save her. Large numbers of awake women taking action, and with the interconnectedness that women are so good at, can change the negative direction the world is headed in.

Margaret Mead's famous quote, "Never doubt that a small

group of committed individuals can change the world, indeed it's the only thing that ever has," is not only inspirational, it's true.

Waiting is an energy that perceives someone or something *outside* us as the source. Being awake is an energy that perceives and experiences the Core Essence Self *within* as the source and the catalyst for action.

We women must stop waiting and wake up, and we must do it in large numbers, and we must do it *now*. This is not a dress rehearsal. It's the proverbial 11th hour. The world needs us to stop being dependent girls and to become awake, powerful women who take initiative and relinquish the destructive energy of waiting.

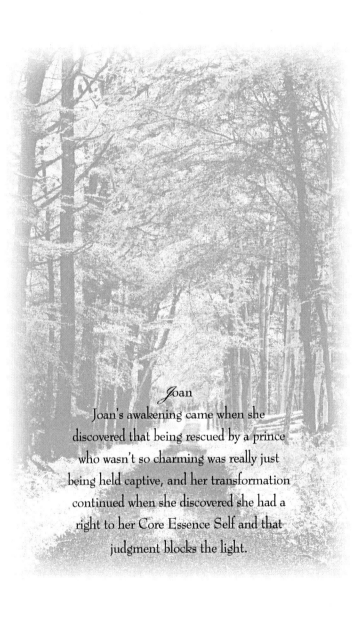

Joan

Joan's awakening came when she
discovered that being rescued by a prince
who wasn't so charming was really just
being held captive, and her transformation
continued when she discovered she had a
right to her Core Essence Self and that
judgment blocks the light.

Joan

Sometimes in your life you will go on a journey.
It will be the longest journey you have ever taken.
It is the journey to find yourself.
—Katherine Sharp

I was married throughout my twenties, and I refer to those years as my time living in a cave. I was completely "unconscious," depressed, and had put on a lot of weight. My world had become very, very small. I was "asleep" so much of my life before that, too, because I'd experienced so much trauma in my life. So, I was really pretty disconnected from myself from very early on. My first major split with myself was at about 18 months old, and then I had some other significant splits at about age five or six, and then the ultimate was when I was 10 and my father started sexually abusing me. Being "awake" would've been like living on another planet. Life was dreary. Making it through a day at a time during my childhood, adolescence and through my twenties was a tremendous struggle.

Things were very difficult before I got married, and I thought that the answer was go get myself a husband and create my own family. I fully expected that *that* was going to be *it*, that everything was going to be better. When I discovered that not only was it *not* better, but at some level, it was much *worse*, that's when I really went even deeper into depression and became even more asleep. He was my hope. I thought that it was going to be *him*, and when I realized that he and the marriage weren't the answer, there was only despair. I had everything leveraged on it working. I couldn't entertain even the possibility that it couldn't work.

My waking up began when I went to a hypnotist to lose weight, and he turned out to be a really good therapist, so I started engaging in therapy. Then my husband started seeing him, too, and then we got into group therapy together. I started connecting with the therapeutic process. That was the beginning of a bit of a wake-up. The big wake-up call came through a crazy woman in the group who was a real troublemaker. She told me that my husband had told her that he had always been waiting for another woman to come along. Hearing that was validation that he really was as unengaged emotionally as he'd been demonstrating to me. So, that was it. That was my breaking point. I came home and told him to leave. He didn't expect me to do that, but I did. That was it for me. I was out of there. I thought, "No, no, I'm not doing this anymore." Once I made that decision, I knew that I was on my own. I had two young children and I had to take care of them and myself. I went back to college to get my degree, but I needed to support us, so I went down to the welfare office. This was all brand new to me. My husband had left, I'd enrolled at the university, and for the next four years I supported the kids and myself on $3500 a year. Even 30 years ago, that was very little. My ex-husband paid less than $40 a month in child support. I met a couple of other single moms and we supported each other so strongly, and we would come up with these innovative ways to find food and get the gas bill paid. A part of my wake-up call was that I was learning that I could take care of myself, and that I could do it under very difficult circumstances. I also learned how incredibly strong I really was, and resourceful. I lost about 50 pounds pretty fast; that's common when women divorce, and I began to eat healthier.

So, my wake-up call was that comment from that woman. Interestingly, when I talked with my ex-husband later, he said, "You know, I never did say that to her. What I said to her was that I always thought that *if* we ever split up, or *if* I ever left you, it would be because of another woman." Well, either way, her comment was exactly what I needed to wake me up so I could move forward.

I had another wake-up call when my son was about five and said to me, "Mommy, why do you cry every day?" That was a huge wake-up call because I thought, "I don't want to be giving my son the message that this is what life is." That comment he made was the catalyst for me to go back into therapy. My waking up process was like a long, arduous climb up a very rocky mountain, and sometimes I would go back "to sleep" a bit.

I kept going because I knew that I didn't have any alternative. I had to take care of my kids. I had to finish my education and begin a career, and I did that. Then, after working for a number of years, I got my Masters. Right before I got my Bachelor's degree, though, I was so exhausted and depleted, and I made a vow to God. I said, "If you will lift this depression, I will make my spiritual path my primary commitment." I became more and more immersed in the world of spiritual concepts and studies. I became a student of *The Course in Miracles*. I went in deep, fast. I took it very seriously. That's how I began picking up a lot of momentum.

There was absolutely no going back at that point. But, I did have a ways to go when it came to relationships. I hadn't awakened too much in that department. I still thought I could find a man to rescue me. I was looking for a savior. There was a man I got involved with who didn't want a relationship. I thought he was my soulmate and didn't want to accept no for an answer. He was a sweet, depressed, little guy. I would attach to obsessions with unavailable men, like him, and that would consume all my energy.

Even after I was divorced and had become good at taking care of myself, I was still committed to the idea that I would find a man to rescue me. I figured I'd just picked the wrong man the first time when I got married. I thought that if I tried hard enough, I could accomplish this. It never happened. I remember the last relationship where I was still thinking about that. It was with a man who's not much of a savior type. He was the most ordinary guy imaginable and probably one of the nicer guys around. It was with him that I finally, completely relinquished the savior fantasy. I thought, "I'm not doing this anymore. It takes too much energy. It's *never* going to happen, and I'm a much better rescuer of myself than anybody I've found so far, anyway." So, I'd finally gotten to the point where I completely gave up the rescue fantasy. But it was years and years after the divorce.

The more I focused on my connection to Spirit, and through many years of therapy, self-discovery, and learning, the more that I experienced that the answers are inside. It was a gradual process that gained momentum. I became more and more adept at turning inside and then trusting what I learned on the inside.

Now I am so much more in the moment. I'm experiencing, enjoying, and living. I am really *living* the mystery. I have a sense of being carried down a river, carried by the energies of life.

These days I am really living my *own* life. I love my work and I feel that what I am doing is valuable because it helps to change lives. I am the artist of my own life and I'm painting quite a portrait. I meditate, I read inspiring and spiritual books. I spend a lot of time with nature, spend time with my dog. I exercise. I do whatever I want to nourish and express myself. My children are grown and I'm very proud of the adults they've become.

1) Joan speaks of being totally asleep much of her life. When have you been most asleep?

2) Joan's wake up calls were very painful. Have there been painful experiences in your life that you can see now as wake up calls?

3) Joan spoke of waking up in some areas and remaining asleep in her need to be rescued. Can you look at your life and see that you are awake in some areas and asleep in others? What are they?

Permission to Rage

In a world that's rapidly catapulting toward disaster, fueled by the dominator model, what do we do with our anger?

The patriarchal system demands that we please others; quiet our voices; and adapt to whatever situation we find ourselves in. In the service of this suppression of our power, we learn to deny our anger or turn it against ourselves.

The following essay is a demonstration of laying claim to my anger and using it to mobilize action. I offer this rant in the energy of Mother Bear fierceness. The niceness and pacifity we've been programmed into no longer serves us or the planet.

Creating a No Bullshit Zone

> When women are depressed they eat or go
> shopping. Men invade another country.
> —Elayne Boosler

When women wake up, we create a "no bullshit zone." Women tolerate so much under the guise of "being nice." I remember that when I was young, my father said about my mother, "She wouldn't say 'shit' if she had a mouthful." What in the world is that? It's bullshit. On the outside, she was the embodiment of the nice mother, good friend, and tolerant wife, and inside she raged.

The patriarchal aspects of bullshit include power and control, waging wars, using weapons of mass destruction as a scare tactic, and cultural tolerance for disrespect, psychological abuse, and domestic violence. Just as bad is the apathy, denial, and tolerance of those women who receive and witness this mindset and treatment and, instead of standing up for themselves, go to the mall, turn on the TV, or embark on the next diet, exercise program or cosmetic surgery.

Our planet is dying and we're shopping.

Now *that's* bullshit.

Male versions of bullshit are everywhere and easy to spot: wars, competition, and disregard for the natural world and human life.

Female versions of bullshit are packaged so attractively:

- "She's so sweet."
- "She's so pretty."
- "She's so nice."
- "Did you see that outfit she had on?"
- "She likes to shop 'til she drops."
- "She wouldn't say 'shit' if she had a mouthful."

In the face of male bullshit, we simply distract ourselves and silence ourselves. That's the female version of bullshit.

Maintaining the mindless shopper or helpless victim stance while watching children starve and the planet die doesn't sit quite right with me. Yes, patriarchy dominates. Yes, women are programmed to submerge and deny their power. But, that has to change. Women must awaken because maintaining the status quo is bullshit.

Many women, especially in America and other Western nations, are enormously privileged. We are well-educated, financially independent, and have healthy bodies and long lives. We have power and we can increase that power through our interconnectedness.

"Gather the Women" is a grassroots organization that was created to support this interconnectedness, and Jean Bolen's "Millionth Circle" is a powerful venue for growing the interconnection and power of women who choose to use their voices and energies to help us all. You can learn more about these and other groups in the Resource Guide at the end of this book.

The opportunities exist, and the choice is there for each one of us to make. Women, wake up and create a "no bullshit zone." We have a world to save.

The Power of Forced Silence

No pressure. No diamonds.
—Mary Cace

Forced silence is like a dam that holds back enormous power. When an energy coursing with enormous momentum, like the life force, is stopped and contained, the stored energy is concentrated and increased by the containment. Having one's voice silenced by the larger culture yields the paradoxical result of strengthening the power of the silenced voice.

I am reminded of the story of the experiment with the frog that had one leg tied down, but the other free to kick at will. The kick response was triggered equally by stimulating the bottom of both feet. Measurements revealed that the frog had developed more strength and muscle mass in the leg that had been held down than the one that had been allowed to move freely.

South African leader Nelson Mandela lived in prison and forced public silence for decades. When he was released, the depth of his message had been clearly and powerfully intensified by his silence. The Quaker religion greatly values silence. Speaking only when one feels prompted from within is part of the basic structure of Quaker meetings.

What goes on beneath the surface in the deep inner recesses of the millions of people, including women, who have been marginalized and silenced by the dominant patriarchal culture? When silenced, the collective energies of those silenced goes underground to gestate. The same process applies to those who have been silenced by trauma and violence. In researching my book about resiliency, *Mining for Diamonds*, I studied the accessing and development of internal resources that might have lain dormant inside people had they not been faced with the sheer necessity of exploring their own inner world to find ways to survive.

This is truly where the riches of your being reside. Psychological abuse, trauma, illness, cultural bondage, and violence force us to shield ourselves from the outside world as we explore this inner world. Buttressed against the dangers of the outside world, we find in our inner world a treasure trove of gifts from our soul. These gifts are not found in the world of form because they exist only *within* us. Emotional and physical hardships are, ironically, some of the most effective vehicles for directing our attention into our inner realms where these treasures are to be found.

The metaphors for the treasures within are everywhere. Jesus said, "The kingdom of Heaven is within you." Teresa of Avila wrote of "the interior castle." Eckert Tolle told a parable of a beggar who sat for years on an old wooden box which, unbeknownst to him, was filled with gold. How ironic that the energies of force, power, control, and dominance that force us to move inward actually provide the catalyst for emerging more powerful than we ever dreamed possible.

Jan

Jan's awakening is a powerful example
of pain as a catalyst for freeing
ourselves, finding the Core Essence
Self, and owning your own brilliance.

Jan

Catastrophe is the essence of the spiritual path,
a series of breakdowns allowing us to discover the
threads that weave all of life into a whole cloth.
—Joan Halifax

I feel like I'm waking up, but I'm not awake. I think that to be awake lies beyond the scope of my lifetime. So, that process of really becoming awake and connected to our spiritual energy is something that is coming. We're awakening but there's a part of us that's still asleep. I can identify a certain part of me that was more asleep than the other parts of me. This was the part that manifested when I attached myself to powerful men, brilliant men, creative men, very headstrong men, and molded myself in the patriarchal image of the complacent woman. I hid my own brilliance behind them by being the helpmate, being the person who had everything under control so the men could shine.

My sleep state has been strongly tied to patriarchal perspectives of what it means to be a woman, a good woman—a woman who hides her bigness, who shrouds her soul and her Spirit so that she doesn't scare away other people, so that she is not as big and bright and shiny as she's been put here on earth to be. My sleeping state has been characterized by a compulsion to be small, to hide, to be silent. That made me feel extreme frustration, discontentment, and anger, repressed anger. I had feelings of never being good enough, smart enough, or worthy enough to be visible; feelings that the gifts that I've been given are there for somebody *else* to use, but not for *me* to use; not for me to heal the planet or heal myself, or to try and heal the people around me. Instead, I believe that the gifts are to be given away for somebody else's agenda. Their agenda might not be healing, or about love, or about connecting to people. It might not be about the things I believe are important or fit with my values. Being asleep hurt so badly.

I was waiting for something to change, but I don't know if I was waiting for somebody to wake me up. I think I was waiting for somebody to soothe me, to love me, to see me. I was waiting to be chosen. I was waiting to be worthy. I was waiting to be filled up from the outside. I was waiting for my pain to subside. I had a lot of problems eating at different points in my life and that's really about being able to feed and nourish yourself. I couldn't do that very effectively at different points in my life. I felt like I was starving. The waiting was about physically, emotionally, and spiritually starving. I was starving for myself.

When you're starving, your body starts to eat its muscle, and you digest yourself. In a way, that's what I felt like I was doing. I was digesting tiny little bits of myself until I was just hollow. I was waiting for something outside me to fill me up. I wasn't aware there was another reality, but I was aware that something was terribly wrong in my life, inside of me, in the world, in the way I was living my life. But if you've never been to another place, you can imagine what that place is like, but you don't have a roadmap to get there. I lacked the skills and the capacity to know what it was like to be on the other side, to know what it was like to have pieces of me awake that had been sleeping for so long. All I knew was that there was just too much pain to live with, so something had to change. I had to somehow pull myself up and find another way to be in the world.

There are countless illustrations of my sleep state, most of them in my relationships with men. I had a long-term relationship many years ago in which I felt utterly silenced. I didn't feel that way in the beginning, but I gave away my voice bit by bit. I gave away my desire, my heart, my gifts, my dreams, my soul, my joy, my meaning, piece-by-piece until there was nothing left to give away.

There were three incidents in that relationship within a very short period of time that made me finally realize that it would *never* be *my* turn. I kept thinking, he's working on his career, he's so smart, he's this, he's that. Soon it will be my turn.

The last of three incidents changed everything. I have a powerful love of animals, and my dog, who I loved deeply, was my best buddy. I had two dogs then, and this one dog was a giant dog and he just laid down beside me one day—and he was only six—and he died. I was pretty shocked. There was no indication that this would happen. It was late at night, and my partner was away on a business trip. A friend's husband, who was a veterinarian, came over right way to help me get this giant dog off the third floor of my house. We laid him down by the front door. My partner came home, opened the door, walked in, and was completely disconnected. Anybody who knows me would know that my dog dying was something that strongly affected me. He came in, looked at the dog, and said, "Oh."

I told him that the dog died. He just said, "Oh," and he paused. He picked up his foot and stepped over my dead dog, who filled up the whole hallway. I watched his foot. It was like in slow motion. It went up into the air, went over my dog's chest, touched the other side of the floor, and he walked up the stairs.

He said something like, "I just have to take off my suit and I'll be down in a few minutes." It was then that I realized that it would *never* be my turn. We were so emotionally disconnected that he could step over my dead dog. With that one step, my *whole* life changed. I started a completely different life path. That was the first wake-up call. It happens in stages.

The final event was again in a relationship with a man who I felt utterly pathologically and emotionally connected to. This was the man after the dog-stepper. I remember trying so hard in that relationship to be silent and supportive, and at the same time more proactive about myself, but old patterns die hard. The wake-up call was that he had a relationship with somebody else. That devastated me. I hadn't actually dealt with the emotions of the breakup of my previous relationship, which had lasted 13 years, and then suddenly this five-year relationship was falling apart. I just wept. I totally lost it. I have a powerful mind. I can create connections very easily, and I can create stories, and I can create things in my mind that explain the way the world is as most people can't. I'd been able to explain away all the feelings of discomfort that I'd had in that relationship for years. I'd tricked myself into thinking it was going to be something else, and that it was worth sticking it out. When it all came apart, there was nothing in my brain that could explain it. I'd been the best I could be, as smart as I could be, as good as I could be, as supportive as I could be, as generous as I could be, as kind as I could be. I'd given everything away again, and it *still* wasn't good enough. I tried desperately to make some sense of this in my brain. I couldn't. There was nothing there except utter confusion. It was a bad week.

I remember feeling suddenly that I was too exhausted to think about anything anymore, and that everything I thought I'd ever known had completely fallen out from underneath me. The only way forward was to not trust anything I had learned before and to start new. I felt sad, angry, great self-loathing, and confusion. So, that's where I started. Start where you're at, and that's where I was at. And I started to rebuild it one piece at a time.

My social mask crumbled. I felt beyond broken. I'd felt broken before and I'd always managed to stick it back together. I could tell myself something to make it work, to make me soldier on, but this time, I was shattered. There was nothing left to piece together. It was a falling away of all the things I'd been told, all the truths that I thought were truth. That's when I realized the only truth is the truth that lies within me. *I'm* the one who knows who I am. I am who I am because of the Universal Spirit that has created me the way I am to bring something to the world. I don't know what it is sometimes, and I'm not sure how it's going to manifest.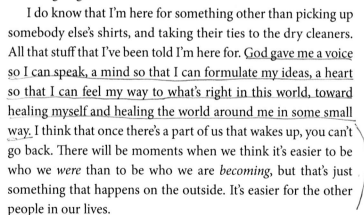

I do know that I'm here for something other than picking up somebody else's shirts, and taking their ties to the dry cleaners. All that stuff that I've been told I'm here for. God gave me a voice so I can speak, a mind so that I can formulate my ideas, a heart so that I can feel my way to what's right in this world, toward healing myself and healing the world around me in some small way. I think that once there's a part of us that wakes up, you can't go back. There will be moments when we think it's easier to be who we *were* than to be who we are *becoming*, but that's just something that happens on the outside. It's easier for the other people in our lives.

We think it's easier to be part of the world we come from, but it isn't. It isn't easier to *not* be who you are becoming because you have so much to push down. The whole waking process is about erupting. And once you've erupted…you can't put the lava back in the volcano. Once the lava hardens, it creates a different appearance on the outside. It creates something that's less penetrable than it was before. So waking up, erupting, is ultimately a strengthening process.

Because I'd been stifled for so long, as the wall came down, as I started to free myself and untie myself, I gained momentum. I was just so elated to be free. I couldn't be contained.

I finished my doctorate, dropped some old business I'd been doing, and dropped many relationships that I'd been involved in. I'd bought another house, and I fixed it up. It was an attempt to make up for years and years of lost self-expression. I started sculpting and writing fiction again. I started painting, which I always wanted to do. I bought a piano. I dug out my guitar and just started playing. Creative energy has sustained my momentum for years.

Today what sustains my momentum is a love of what I do. I enjoy connecting with like-minded people who aren't afraid to be who they are. Being with these people supports my awakening and I find it truly inspiring.

 I'm a high introvert. I can spend a lot of time alone. I think it's because I've been alone most of my life. Even when I've been in intimate relationships with men I've been alone. So, I'm good at being alone. My quest now is to find ways to build community and to maintain my own integrity within that community. I have tons of energy, ideas, and creative spirit, so it's not hard for me to give all that away. I'm realizing that if you give it all away you have to engage in a thorough self-care program. I'm not good at that yet, but I'm getting better. I think the journey in life is forward. You can go sideways a bit, but there is no back.

There's a lot of stuff in our world that encourages women to wait to be rescued, and I think women are really good at that. If you're asleep or partly asleep, your life is really like a dream. And a dream is something we observe from the outside as if we're not a player, as if we're not in our own dreams. In a dream we're not self-directed. We've been socialized to sleep, and to believe that in many ways our life doesn't begin until we're chosen by somebody.

When we're chosen, we're chosen according to how well we fit into *their* plan. So, the idea is to be as much of a blank slate as possible, to literally be a sleeping object of desire, but to have no self-direction. It's like decorating a house. If the house is beige and you put in some nice furniture but it's all neutral, it's going to appeal to more people than if you have red walls and a crazy velvet couch. Be as neutral as possible, we've been taught, and you will be chosen. Be as neutral as possible and you can fit into as many other lives as possible. That's when you exercise your acrobatic abilities. Fit into somebody's life, Presto-change-o, now you're this. Presto-change-o, now you're that. Watch me, I can bend this way. Watch me, I can bend that way. Women do this all the time. We've been taught to serve and please, but, at what cost? The destruction of Self. At the cost of living our life in a dream state.

I think this is a fundamentally spiritual journey. When all is lost, you have to go to the *one* thing, the *last* thing you have, that *cannot* be lost—and that's the kernel of the Self that lies within each one of us. The tiny little piece that you haven't given away yet.

It starts with the question, "What is left? What do I have inside me?" Then you ask, "How do I grow that?" I recognized the piece inside of me that couldn't be destroyed. I discovered that it was stronger than everything I'd faced and everything I'd learned. It's the strength of the universe. It's the strength that connects us. It's the strength of the Great Spirit. It's me, but it's not me. It's the life-force that we all share, and that's the starting point.

Now every day feels better than the last. Every day I feel more connected and have a deeper awareness of self than I did the day before. I'm more grounded than I've ever been. I'm stronger and more self-aware than I've ever been. When we really have that strength inside we can let go of ego and our image. We can let go of the material trappings around us and just experience the emotion and bliss of life. We can experience the connection between our minds, the great tool that they are, our hearts, the great compass that they are, and our bodies, the most amazing vehicles that they are.

My life has changed so much since I've been more awake. I'm much happier, too. I'm closer to my path than ever, and everyday I get closer.

1) Jan speaks about hiding her brilliance, making herself small. In what ways do you do that?

2) Jan speaks about the frustration of not having a road map to get to a new place. How do you see the stories of the awakening women included in the book as a road map?

3) Jan compares the waking up process to the eruption of a volcano. How does that metaphor apply to your life?

The Cosmic Choir

We are each gifted in unique in important ways.
It is our privilege and our adventure to
discover our own special light.
—Mary Dunbar

We live in a universe of energy, and we are made up of energy. We are co-creators of our own reality because the concepts we plug into are literally the energy fields we are living in. These once esoteric concepts have now become familiar catch phrases: What you think about expands, and where your attention goes, your energy flows. If we all really understood this, and lived accordingly, how conscientious we'd be about where we direct our thoughts and our energy!

More than 15 years ago, I had an experience that I never forgot. I was lying down in a meditative state and the phrase "thoughts are things" hit my consciousness like the proverbial lightning bolt. From that point on, I've been conscious of how I direct my thoughts. I know their power. Spiritual leaders have long taught The Law of Attraction, the idea that we actually attract our experiences into our lives, that we co-create our reality with the other energies in the universe. Now, with the publication of the bestselling book, *The Secret*, this concept, written about for many years in so many previous books, is finally becoming mainstream. The understanding that we are energetic beings in an energetic universe has been scientifically explained by our increased understanding of quantum physics, and we're finally beginning to accept and implement this in our lives.

Each of the women whose experiences show us the way, has moved through not only a process of exploring and connecting with her inner world, but also the process of realizing that each of us has an energetic connection to everyone and everything else in the universe. They have learned that the inner connection and universal connectedness shine a light on their own unique purpose. Several of the women actually told me, "It's as if there's a great cosmic orchestra, and each of us has our own part to play."

Each woman demonstrated that the more intimately and completely we know ourselves; the more clear we become in the knowing and expression of that inner essence; the way we live our lives; the more clear we are about the part we play in the cosmic orchestra, the part we sing in the cosmic choir.

Waking Up is Hard Work

You must do the thing you think you can not do.
—Eleanor Roosevelt

As a therapist, I work with women on both ends of the self-awareness spectrum. A woman who lived at one end of that spectrum—only in the material outer world—was the embodiment of the woman asleep. Her activities and attentions were limited to shopping, housecleaning, watching television, and alternately trying to please her husband and children and trying to get them to change. She didn't work outside the home, and struggled with "finding her passion."

The unfortunate reality was that she was so entrenched in focusing outward and denying her inner world that finding her passion was completely impossible. The source of the passion lies on the inside, and her inside was a place she was definitely not going to explore.

At the other end of the self-awareness spectrum was the woman who worked very hard for several years excavating and clearing her inner realms. This woman worked through the effects of many years of childhood trauma, abusive relationships, and alcohol addiction. As she cleared these blocks in her inner world, she became progressively more clear that she was a healer. That was her passion. Her connection to her Core Essence Self became so well developed that the people she worked with were tremendously impacted by her energy. She would never have been able to access these high vibrations had she not worked through her issues and cleared her inner realms.

The first woman, mired in the mundane, is a woman who not only hasn't cleaned off the facets of her diamond, she is busily engaged in accumulating more and more debris on her beautiful diamond Core Essence Self. Her part in the cosmic choir may never be sung because she is frittering away her life force obsessing about the superficial.

The second woman worked diligently to clean the debris off the facets of her diamond and now it shines brilliantly. The light of her diamond lights her own life, but it also lights the lives of those she helps to heal, which is her part in the cosmic choir.

Two lives, two choices. Two very different outcomes.

The choice to stay asleep.

The choice to wake up.

Healing Yourself, Healing the Earth

Heaven is under our feet as well as over our heads.
—Henry David Thoreau

I take long walks in the woods with my dog, Daisy. Those of us on a spiritual path and also living in the dog world have an agreed upon belief that "our dog finds us to teach us what we need to learn." Daisy has been a blessing and a challenge since she chose me at the Humane Society. She's a herding breed, so she thinks it's her job to herd me. I guess it is.

Walking Daisy (or more accurately, Daisy walking *me*) has given me a connection to Mother Earth that I might not have made otherwise. I have fallen in love with Mother Earth. A friend who is a committed mediator told me that if you're quiet enough you can hear Mother Earth scream. If I were Mother Earth, I'd scream, too. How can she *not* be in pain? Like any loving mother, she provides unlimited nurturing, but like spoiled, thoughtless children, we only take and take, and we're on the brink of destroying her. Where is our love, respect, and gratitude for our Mother Earth who continues to give us so much?

As women, we can relate to Mother Earth's plight. As we love her more by actively connecting with her, we move ourselves into more authentic power. As women, we've bought into the passive energy of waiting to be taken care of by men whom we've made the source and central figures in our lives as we sit passively by while the planet we literally depend upon for our existence is defiled and headed for destruction. But, when we love Mother Earth, that energy can reverse the destructive trajectory.

Every dawn is the beginning of a new day on the planet and in our lives. When women wake up, it's also the beginning of a new day. Recognizing and claiming the dawn is an integral part of waking up. When we're awake, we have a story. We create one. When we are asleep and living under the spell of a patriarchal culture, we do not create our own story. Instead, we play the supporting role in his story. Put those two words together and you get *history*. We literally do *not* want history to repeat itself.

When I work with women who are co-dependent in a relationship, I point out to them, "When you live your life focused on *him*, he gets *two* lives, and you don't get any." Women go to various gatherings, groups, and meetings to vent about men, but how often do they awaken from their co-dependency? How often do they instead just sit there day after day, week after week, some even year after year, and complain about "his" behavior while remaining dependent and never taking responsibility for their own lives?

What would happen if "she" woke up and claimed her own power and her own life? She would open her eyes and look at the world, and breathe in the life force. Then stand up on her own and go out into that world. Alone, if that's what it takes. What a different energy than sleeping through the dawns of her life, waiting for a man to give her the kiss of resurrection, and then spending her life living only *his* life.

Often we are assisted in our awakening by energies of

acceptance. I remember years ago when I received my acceptance letter from the University of Michigan. I opened it, read it and screamed. I began jumping up and down and running around in circles. The energies that this experience called forth were the energies of acceptance, forward movement, and opportunity. I felt—*I knew*—that I could do whatever I wanted to do. This letter was an open door to my potential, my potential to access a powerful vehicle that would assist me in offering my gifts to the world. It was enormous "I can do it" energy.

This was, and is, the energy of awakened women.

Living in the Moment

Lightness of touch and living in the moment are intertwined. One can not dance well unless one is completely in time with the music, not leaning back to the last step or pressing forward to the next one, but poised directly on present step as it comes.

—Anne Morrow Lindbergh

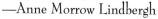

Energies flow toward us, through us, and with us. One day, I decided I'd try a Zen approach to writing. So, I sat down and wrote with no thought about the past or the future. I only wrote in the moment, connecting with the inner spaciousness and allowing my unconscious mind to connect to my writing arm.

What happened then was amazing.

I trusted.

I allowed the words to flow out of my pen. I brought myself back to the moment whenever I strayed. I held on to the moment. And guess what happened next?

Inspiration came.

It came like a flitting butterfly. It was here and then it was gone. I caught a glimpse of it, and then it moved on. I thought that if I became even more still and silent it would light on me.

It did.

That took trust and a willingness to release each moment as it came and went.

Living without attachment, immersed in the moment, trusting, releasing, and flowing, yields a different energy than the energy of the controlling step-by-step process of the Western world.

When we are awake, we can flow with the energies of the moment. When we are awake, these energies *can* flow because we are not blocked. And because we are not blocked, we can also feel, receive, and transmit the energy of love, the light of love.

Lani

Lani's awakening was reached through the doorway of education. She shows us that knowledge is learned, but wisdom is divine prompting from within.

Lani

Risk! Risk anything! Care no more for the opinions of others, for those voices. Do the hardest thing on earth for you. Act for yourself.
—Katherine Mansfield

In my childhood, I was aware of events and things around me, but I wasn't awake in the sense of knowing that I had free will and choice. Other people were in charge, my parents or other people around me, affecting my life.

When I was eight or nine, I was sexually assaulted by some acquaintances of my parents at a sleepover with their daughter, whom I really didn't know well. I think they drugged me. I remember not being able to move and it being hard to physically wake up. It was a pretty intense experience. I didn't fully remember it until about five or six years ago because I'd blocked it out. It was important to remember, even the painful parts, to fully own it and bring it into my consciousness.

With fairy tales, little girls imagine a prince or some sort of magical event, where someone or something will rescue you. But, in my heart, I knew that just wasn't going to happen and that fairy tales were fairy tales. Even though I enjoyed them, I learned pretty early on that it was up to me to get things done.

I felt trapped, but I knew that it was up to me to rescue myself when I was young. I had a boyfriend when I was six years old. We'd play different games, like house, and one time we played a game where he had to rescue me…and he never showed up.

He had been called home to do something, so he never showed up. And that was a really good thing, actually, for me to realize early on that there wasn't going to be some man or some hero or someone else who was going to rescue me. I was going to have to find a way out myself. It was disappointing at the time, but in retrospect it was a good thing that he never showed up.

My wake up call happened in high school. I was a good student, and in my junior year, I realized that I'd better get on with it if I wanted to make something of my life. I'd gained a lot of weight as a child in reaction to the assault. It was a way of staying asleep or safe. So, also when I was about 16, I realized that I was physically out of shape and I'd better get fit. I also started to really pursue the things that I enjoyed, which included writing, reading, and working with other people. I wanted to learn about life, to travel, to study. I really blossomed when I became a junior in high school.

I wanted to be happy, and I could see that it was in my hands to do that. If I didn't do it, I'd really regret it and I'd be very unhappy. I didn't want that. I could see the results of that in my family, of things and events that they had never fully come to terms with.

Something else happened as a wake-up call. I'm a very good swimmer, but one time when I was 17, I was swimming on the North Shore of O'ahu and got caught in a riptide. Fortunately, I was slammed onto the shore by a wave. Otherwise, I wouldn't have made it. I almost died that day, and I realized that it was time I really started figuring out what I was going to do with my life.

I had another traumatic, but empowering experience that same year in high school. I had some really great teachers, but I also had one very bad teacher who was only there for a year. I don't know what was going on in her life, but whatever it was really impacted her ability to be objective and teach well. At the end of my senior year, she was going to fail me even though I'd been averaging an A the entire time and had worked very hard. That was incredibly unfair, and I wasn't going to allow it to happen.

So, I went to the principal and complained about the teacher. Only one other student in the class would do that, and that was my sister. None of the other students spoke up. One parent of one of the students complained. Later, I found out that more people complained after my sister and I had. I felt very alone, but I also felt that I needed to do it. I went to the principal and explained the situation, and later I met with the teacher and she threatened me and attacked my character, and I went back to the principal.

It was traumatizing, but it was also very empowering because I realized that stuff was going to happen and people are who they are, but it's up to me how I'm going to react in the face of injustice. It was a real turning point for me, recognizing that just because an adult is an adult, it doesn't mean that they're looking out for your well being.

Now, in life I make that choice over and over. I can let it run me over, I can run away from it, or I can deal with it. These difficult experiences empowered me to accept things, events and people as they are and to take positive action.

Education has been the key for me in terms of self-esteem and in getting the information that I needed. It's been the key to becoming who I am. Not being aware is almost like death, maybe worse than death.

I've been awakening in an upward spiral ever since, but there have been times when I've gone back to sleep for a while because it's too painful to be fully awake, especially after a series of losses one right after the other. In college I drank too much on weekends and, even though I kept my grades up, it affected my better judgment, and I was involved in several unfulfilling relationships. I got that under control after graduation, but it came up again eight years later, when my back was injured. I have been recovering from that injury over the past decade, as well as alcoholism, workaholism, and depression related to chronic pain. Finally, around 9/11, when we were all traumatized, I also lost my work, several close friends, relatives and relationships important to me. These were very dark times in my life.

Yet, I'm fully awake now, and I've found some equilibrium and support that I didn't have before. Ironically, it was because of the most painful moments of my life that I began to find worth in all parts of myself, including the "negative" or "bad" parts. I had also cultivated other ways of bringing myself into balance, including *vipassana,* insight meditation, *metta*, loving-kindness meditation, therapy, exercise, rest, meaningful work and love.

I didn't seek to be rescued, I knew that it's up to me. I get up and keep going. It's about pulling myself up by my bootstraps, but there are other sources of support out there. One of those is my husband, and I have some very good friends I've known for years and I have spiritual sources I call on to help me see things clearly, to help me move forward. But ultimately, it's up to me to make these choices and move forward and really live.

It's not just me against the world; it's really about whether I chose to be a strong link. The Buddha says that each person needs to nurture his or her own link and make it strong. Then they link up with other links in the chain. We're responsible for keeping ourselves healthy and strong, and for connecting with others and helping them to keep themselves healthy and strong. There's a Divine plan as to why we're here.

Along the way I realized it was also a matter of reaching out for help and support and being open, and also understanding that not everybody can provide that. We're really interconnected and not alone. I don't have to be invincible. It's not possible to do that. I can rely on certain people, and I can also provide support for them. That inspired me to create co-empowerment workshops in 2005. There's something magical and powerful about a group of people helping each other find insight and ways to empower themselves and support other people.

When you believe the answer is outside you, it's like seeing things as a child, where everything is determined for you, or you think it is. As you continue to grow you become more of an adult and more independent. When you're fully awake, it's taking a further step, towards interdependence. It's about connecting with others and about noticing that external events happen and we make conscious choices about how we let them impact us internally. You transcend them.

There are external things and events, other people over whom I don't have control, but I have control over what I make of them in my life, and that's very comforting. I feel stronger now than I ever have and more interconnected. I am connecting with people who support my life mission, and whose missions I can support. I also understand that there are people who are in alignment with what I'm doing and others who are not. The energy of interconnectedness is a very creative thing, but there are people who mistake force for power and use that to destroy.

People are waking up to realize that it's important that we create something better, something collaborative, because the other way leads to the death of ourselves and the planet. The key is to find what each of us can do and then connect with each other to make it happen.

My calling is to help people who are going through transitions to empower themselves. It's energizing, exciting, and exhilarating. I come alive when I'm doing co-empowerment workshops.

I nourish and nurture my relationship with myself in many ways. I take time daily to meditate and to write in my journal. I take care of myself physically: strength training, yoga, cardiovascular exercise, nutrition and rest. I forgive myself and others for our human weaknesses and focus upon our strengths.

1) Lani speaks about seeing the answer outside yourself as more childlike and dependent. In what ways do you trust yourself and in what ways don't you trust yourself?

2) Lani told of speaking truth to authority figures and her fear of it. Can you remember times you took a difficult stand and how it turned out?

3) Lani quotes the Buddha who says, "We each need to nurture our own link in the chain and keep it strong." How do you nurture your own link?

Embodying Love

It's so clear that you have to cherish everyone. I think
that's what I get from these older black women, that every
soul is to be cherished, that every flower is to bloom.
—Alice Walker

Love is an energy field that exists everywhere. When we embody love, we bring love into the world's energy and allow it to permeate the denser matter of our bodies.

A friend told me an amazing story. An acquaintance of hers was a man in the final stages of alcoholism. His wife had left him, so he moved in with his 80-year-old mother. He didn't have a driver's license, so one night, he walked to a nearby bar. Many hours later, at about 3:00 a.m., a stranger came to the door of the alcoholic's mother's house carrying her son in his arms. She let him in, and although he'd never been there before, he walked up to her son's bedroom as if he knew exactly where he was going. He laid her son on the bed face up and said, "We're all children of God," and walked out the door.

Her son was dead.

When I heard this story, I felt a wave of chills go through me as my friend and I said in unison, "He was an angel."

We all embody love all the time, but we often forget who we are. Clearly, the alcoholic man was no less a child of God, as the angel who brought him home reminds us.

We are made of the essence of love and only our lack of belief in this stands in our way of experiencing it.

Sandy

Sandy's awakening shows us the power
of silence. When you're still and take
the time to move into the silent place
within yourself; only then will you
locate your Core Essence Self, your
internal source of power.

Sandy

What we're all striving for is authencity,
a Spirit to Spirit connection.
—Oprah Winfrey

My father passed away when I was 25, and he'd always been very supportive and encouraging. When he died, I went through the grief process. I was angry. I was sad. I was lonely. My anger extended to not only my father for leaving me, but to God and my belief system, and I questioned it.

An awareness of angels came into my thoughts. My mind shifted and I kept wondering, "Are there angels? If there are, why aren't they here to help me?" I had all these questions.

I saw in a local magazine that there was going to be an angel seminar, so I signed up and went by myself. Up to that point, I didn't do much by myself. I was always in a group. This was a door opening for me. That's where I began my real spiritual path.

It was an all-day seminar, and there were about 50 people there, in addition to the woman who ran the seminar. At lunchtime, my heart was beating so fast I thought I was having a heart attack. My whole body was vibrating. The woman who led the seminar was walking to lunch and she stopped and looked at me. We'd never met. She said, "You'll work for me some day." I looked at her and said, "I think I'm having a heart attack." She said, "No, that's the energy, the vibrations you're feeling. You'll be fine," and she walked away very casually. I looked at this woman and thought she was crazy.

Then, I went to her four-week seminar and I learned a lot, grew a lot, read all kinds of books. I'd go into Borders and books would fall off the shelf and I'd grab them. Her secretary was leaving and she needed someone to work part-time. I worked at a university full-time and I had no intention of quitting. I went to work for her a couple of nights a week so I could still work my regular job, and I did eventually end up working for her full-time. I started taking classes through someone else and my spiritual awareness really blossomed.

I'm a very analytical, organized person, but I stepped out of that box. Never before had I made a split-second decision, and I began to make them. I was just being pulled into it. I was a little resistant at first, but then I began to flow with what life brought me. So, although my father's death was really sad for me, it was also an opening.

I would say that was my wake up call. I could no longer lean on my father. He wasn't there for me to call and ask what I should do. So where do I turn now? I turned within. I learned that when your support person goes away, it's really for your growth.

That's how you grow within yourself. It forces you to look in and ask help from your own guidance. What the guidance in Spirit would like us to learn is that if we allow it to enter in, co-exist and work with us, it can make our life so much better. They will give us messages. They do so much. We just have to allow them to come in.

Now I have periods of what I call a void. When I asked my spiritual teacher why I'm not getting anything at those times, he said it's because I have the information and now it takes time to be absorbed, that it's increasing my vibrational rate. The more knowledge you get, the more your body's vibrational rate changes. This then changes your frame of mind. That will shift you to another quest. When you need the down time, Spirit gives it to you. I learned not to be frustrated and to work with that. When I didn't feel as in touch with Spirit, I'd meditate, I'd write. Sometimes, I'd move through the void being still and not meditate for months. Then I'd feel that I should meditate. That feeling was Spirit telling me, "It's time, now." There are periods when you feel disconnected and out of the flow, but it's for your own good. It's a time for you to rest.

I stay connected through meditation and communication with my guidance, going to a seminar or classes, and I also go to church where I give messages and sermons from the podium. All of that keeps the channel open. Discipline is the number one accelerator on your spiritual path.

There is a big awakening when we stop trying, because we usually try to find somebody to make us happy, to take care of us. On this path, you realize you don't need someone else. People use judgment, and with that judgment, they'll control you, and manipulate you, and we allow it. Once you realize that *you* have control, then it's not necessary to rely on others. You stand taller, more confident. Your self-esteem comes back, and then you're able to prepare when people come at you about things because you're stronger.

One of the changes as I'm waking up is that there isn't a pessimistic part of me, ever. I'm always optimistic. I feel like I'm more uplifting to everyone. I don't think I've smiled more in all my life.

How I look at life has changed, also how I view it through *my* eyes. Time is more precious to me, and the special moments with my loved ones. I always put love into everything, from cooking to a gentle touch to a conversation. I don't have the anger I used to have. When you feel love, you can't have anger.

Now I take time for myself. I also want to make my physical self feel good so that I can penetrate deeper into myself, so I'll do special things for myself. I take quiet time, too. I step away from my world. That's my main thing.

1) The death of Sandy's father was her wake up call. Have there been losses in your life that have been turning points for you?

2) Sandy speaks of guidance from Spirit. Do you experience yourself asking for help or guidance from unseen forces? Have you ever explored this and what can you discover?

3) Sandy states discipline is the number one accelerator on your spiritual path. What are spiritual practices you use now? What would you like to add?

Standing Up

As a woman I have no country. As a
woman my country is the whole world.
—Virginia Woolf

When women wake up, they stand up and form a matrix of love that heals them and heals the planet. We must all understand the significance and symbolism of the power of standing up.

On a recent Mother's Day, a worldwide initiative requested that women "stand up for peace" at 1:00 p.m. for five minutes. The image and archetype of Sleeping Beauty is the antithesis of standing in one's own power. Sleeping Beauty is lying down, protected from the world, encased in a glass coffin, lost in the forest, waiting for a kiss from the prince who will carry her off in his arms into *his* world.

It's time for the energy of this archetype to be transformed into the energy of a woman standing in her *own* power embracing the world. The energy of standing rather than lying down, waking rather than sleeping, and acting rather than waiting, is an energy that takes us out of the passivity of believing that power lies with men, and that we have no more power than to pretty ourselves up, sit quietly by the phone and wait for him to chose us to be brought into his world and be used for his purposes.

73

It's time for women to say *no* to the restrictive roles that have kept them powerless and asleep, and say *yes* to themselves.

It's time for women to wake up, stand up, extend their energy, love, and light, and make the entire world *theirs* to love and to heal.

Staying Connected

Life is either a daring adventure or nothing at all. Security
is mostly a superstition. It does not exist in nature.
—Helen Keller

We start out as little girls being connected with ourselves. Creative play and physical movement originate on the inside, and when we're engaging in these activities we're not looking to an outside source to fill us up and we're not waiting for approval from another.

When we stop playing and move our attention from self-expression to a focus on physical appearance, we begin relinquishing our connection with ourselves. The life force begins to dim as we move our attention toward attracting a partner, a Prince Charming, who then becomes the focus of our attention. How do I look? How can I please him? How can I find the right man?

The age at which young girls do this appears to be getting progressively younger as our culture has been sexualizing images of girls through the media at progressively younger and younger ages. It's become common to see mainstream entertainment images of six-year-old girls dancing and cheerleading in gyrating, slithering stripper choreography while provocatively dressed in outfits also formerly reserved only for strippers and adult female exotic dancers.

The media-driven focus on appearance and objectifying females is creating a disconnection from Self in even pre-school age girls. "How do I look?" rather than "What am I doing?" becomes the central focus for young girls, and then is encouraged to continue throughout their lives. They are trained to believe that "If I look good, it doesn't matter what I do or don't do."

When this shift from Self to "him" occurs, it's a path that is culturally encouraged, but tragically disappointing for women. The 10-step process goes like this:

1) The little girl plays, creates, and experiences life.

2) Even before she's a teen, she is programmed to consider her search for "him" to be her life's mission, so she prioritizes everything in her life accordingly. She stops playing, creating, and experiencing her own life.

3) As a teen, she embarks on the diligent search for "him."

4) She finds "him," and either entices him to marry her or succumbs to his pressure to marry her.

5) She has a husband whom she focuses all of her attention on, believing that if she can make him happy, she'll automatically be happy. Her husband expects her life to revolve around supporting his endeavors in the world, expects her to be "the woman behind the man," though he is not socialized to reciprocate.

6) She has a home that also requires her constant attention and energy to maintain.

7) She has children who require her attention and energy.

8) If she has a job, she must also meet the needs of her boss.

9) She never gets to focus on herself again. Her energies are completely exhausted by the needs and desires of others. She lives the rest of her life last on the priorities list.

10) She dies, although in many ways she's felt spiritually dead for years.

A study by sociologist Jessie Bernard showed that of the four combinations of marriage and gender, the order of happiness was as follows:

- Most Happy—Single Women
- 2nd Most Happy—Married Men
- 3rd Most Happy—Single Men
- Least Happy—Married Women

The 10-step process I outlined is not the complete picture of marriage for all women, but the passive roles women play as members of a patriarchal, misogynistic culture contribute to an environment that significantly disempowers women and leaves married women as the Least Happy in the Bernard study.

Cassandra

Cassandra's awakening was triggered
by her determination not to have her
life defined by a tragic event, not to
allow her identity to be determined by
other people, and not to seek validation
outside herself.

Cassandra

Invest in the human soul. Who knows,
it might be a diamond in the rough.
—Mary McLeod Bethune

When I was 14, I was raped walking home from school by a
boy in my class. At that point, I was a straight-A student on the
honor roll. I was "asleep" before I was raped. I wanted to be a virgin until I got married. I would've gone on to be just like society
wanted me to be.

After I was raped, I didn't tell anybody because I was ashamed,
and I thought that my mother would think it was my fault because her sex talk was basically, "Don't be a tramp." So, my thing
was that I was going to be a good girl. I'm gonna be smart, I'm
gonna stay a virgin. After I was raped, I kept it a secret. Can you
imagine a 14-year-old child not being able to tell anyone something that horrible? When I got home from school late that day,
I told my parents that two high school girls beat me up. So, for
years I was "asleep" after the rape, too, when I couldn't talk about
it. I went from being a straight-A student to straight Fs. I drank
Southern Comfort and ginger ale every morning. The neighbors
and my family were asking, "God, what happened to her? She
was such a good girl. She was so smart."

I couldn't talk about it because he had asked me for a kiss, and I felt that it was my fault because I went behind the building to give him a kiss and he raped me. I didn't finish high school, but I did complete my GED, and then went to community college, and then to a university. When I was 20, maybe 21, I was writing a paper about marital rape, I read a passage from the book where the woman was describing what it felt like to be raped and I had a breakdown. I started crying and they had to take me to the hospital, and I talked to a psychiatrist. This was the wake-up call. I'd been holding this really dark secret. I was still trying to be a good girl. I told my mother, but it still didn't get any better.

What bothered me the most was what he'd said to me. I remember him telling me that he hated the gap between my teeth and he hated that I was black. That stuck with me. I remember asking him why he was doing this, and I told him that I wanted to wait until I was married and please don't do this. He said, "Nobody is ever going to want you." That's the stuff that really screws you up in your mind. Later I went back and I had a conversation with him in my mind. I had to reclaim myself. I had to tell him that I'm a good person. After I did that I started to really wake up. I still had to deal with my mother's perception of me. I don't think parents understand how damaging it is to only tell a kid, "Don't be a tramp." In my mind, I was thinking I was ruined. I was nothing. After the rape, I'd gone through a period where I had sex, and I got pregnant when I was 15 and I had an abortion. I was a very lost little girl. Before I woke up, all of the secrecy, the promiscuousness, the drinking, were all related to my not being able to talk about it and wanting to fit the image of the good girl. I couldn't do it anymore. Women sometimes feel that we can either be a good girl or a bad girl, but there's nothing in between.

How do you go back to being a good girl? I felt that if I'd really been a good girl, I wouldn't have wanted to kiss a boy. I felt it was my fault, like I deserved it. I felt like my mother would tell me that I'd deserved it.

But, thank God for that experience, because God gave me compassion for other people. When I finally woke up and I got my degrees, I worked as a social worker for years. My clients would look at me and say, "You don't understand," and I would say, "Oh, baby, I *understand*." I understand people at a very deep level. I feel like some of the deepest, most important lessons I learned weren't in textbooks and classrooms. They were from that time in my life. God taught me compassion, understanding, and patience. God taught me how to communicate and love and be a nonjudgmental person. Those things can't be taught. They come from experience. I think that's why I've been a very effective teacher. I teach full time at a community college, and I feel like my greatest gift is my ability to relate to people at so many different levels and from so many different backgrounds. That's because of that period in my life. I didn't feel that way at the time, but I feel that way now.

I don't look for a man now to rescue me, but I have different version of being rescued. I call it the Modern Cinderella Complex. This is a joke with my friends and family. I'd answer the phone like I'm waiting for Oprah to call. It's a joke, but it was true—Oprah calls and my life is gonna change. I was waiting to be saved, waiting for Oprah to come and anoint me and bless me. In the past, women wanted Prince Charming to come on the white horse. Now people think Oprah's gonna make their life great. They're gonna get on her show and everything in their life is going to be okay.

I started a magazine a few years ago and I realized that I was just *looking* busy, hoping that Oprah would call. I wasn't serious. I didn't know I wasn't serious, though. I wasn't marketing myself properly. I thought I needed to look busy and Oprah is gonna find my magazine and call me up and my life is gonna be wonderful. In the last few months I've decided that Oprah *isn't* going to make me, that I'm going to make *myself*. I'm very disciplined now. I've self-published three books.

I think it's important for people to know that when you wake up it gets worse before it gets better. You wake up to this whole new life and this whole new perception of yourself. You need to find a way to adjust to that new reality. It was difficult to integrate my past with my new Self. I didn't see myself as a victim, but as a person who was working on her bachelor's degree. I didn't want to fall into a victim mentality. I didn't want my life story to be about some little black girl who was raped behind the church. I didn't want that to be my story. Being a college student and earning good grades was what really changed my perception of myself. I needed school. It wasn't about getting grades, it was about creating this new image of myself—a young woman who was strong and powerful and believed in herself. I finally felt in control. School was a way for me to prove my own worth to myself.

I got married and had children, and after my divorce, my mother begged me to drop out of school. She said, "Those universities are made out of bricks and stones and they'll be around when you're dead, but your kids are only going to be young for a small period of time and you're going to miss their childhood. So, you need to drop out of school and go back when your kids are older."

I was thinking, oh my God, I'm making $21,000 a year as a

social worker with a Masters degree and I'm struggling. How am I going to provide for my kids? I prayed to God for guidance. I went to school the next day. I was telling a woman in my class that I was about to drop out because of my kids, and she told me not to drop out now when the kids are really small. She said that at that age all they need are Pampers, a bottle, and somebody to play with them and anybody can do that. But, she said, "If you miss their first dance recital or a little league game, they'll never forget." She said that as kids get older their lives get more complex and they need their parents more. For me, she was an angel. That was my answer from God, and I'm so glad I listened. Because it worked for me. I think that if you really pay attention, there are wake-up calls every single day of your life. I didn't drop out, I continued working on my next degree.

I had a serious wake up call last summer. The union said we couldn't teach more than 21 credit hours in a week. That meant I'd have no income for two months in the summer. They could've notified me sooner. It wasn't what they did, it was the way they did it and how it left me without an income. I took it personally, but it was happening to everyone, and my department chair kept reminding me that according to the student evaluations, I was the number one professor at the school. She thought she was soothing me, but it just made me cry harder because I was thinking that if I'm giving everything to my job how could they not take all of this into consideration? I didn't know that a part of me was asleep then. There was still this person inside of me who just wanted to write, and I had told her to shut up and go away. I had to do this and this for my job. But, the same month that I found out I'd have no income for two months, I woke up and I started a magazine. I wasn't angry anymore. I'd awakened to my true Self who wanted to write. I was happy with my job, but I still wanted to write. Now I feel whole. I'm still dedicated to my job, but I also have my magazine and books and I feel I'm being true to myself. I'd been giving to the job the way women give to their husbands, and they put their dreams on hold.

I stay on my path by knowing I didn't want to say could've, would've, should've. That inspired me. The other thing was what our union president told me: "You must remember that those things in life that protect you also limit you. Don't ever forget that." Talk about a wake-up. After this whole thing happened with the college, I told myself that I was never going to give myself like that again. I always buy materials for my students out of pocket. I have a big seminar every semester where I bring in superintendents, principals, and teachers from all over this area. I said to myself, no more of that because that's not in my job description. Well, this prestigious university called me to ask me to teach a class because they'd heard about me. This made me cry. I cried like a fool. The guy who called said they'd heard nothing but wonderful things about me. I thought, this was God saying, "You don't work for that community college, you work for *me*. You work for your spirit. You do your best because that's who you are. It has nothing to do with your job." I'd never in my life gotten a job on my reputation, or had somebody call me and say, "Hey, I want you," without a resume and an interview. They wanted me because of my reputation. That was God. I told myself that no matter what, I would never *not* give less than 100 percent. That keeps me going. Now, if Oprah called me, it wouldn't be because I need her to make me who I am, it would be because I'm already who I am and I'm gonna bring something to her show.

I feel like I just woke up for real. I'm so productive and I'm keeping promises to myself, to my Spirit. That's the best feeling in the world. I just think that the only power that we ever really have is when we do it ourselves.

1) Cassandra's sexual assault seemed to be the worst thing that could happen to anyone, but proved to be the greatest catalyst for growth. What one incident in your life seemed to be the worst tragedy, but yielded the most growth?

2) Cassandra states when you wake up it gets worse before it gets better. How have you grown in response to pain?

3) Cassandra learned that those things that protect you also limit you. In what ways do you take risks and what ways do you cling to security?

Return to the Self

No person is your friend who demands
your silence, or denies your right to grow.
—Alice Walker

We return to the Self when we take the hours we spend on materialistic externals, such as shopping, as well as focusing on other distractions, and move that energy into developing a relationship with our Self. The choices are enormous, and once you make a choice to return to the Self, a different energy field opens up. The return is an active process that changes our trajectory. Our attention is focused in a completely different direction, so energy moves toward the Self and no longer exclusively toward others. This choice opens up monumental power.

Being asleep is like being on automatic pilot. It's like sleep-walking, being a robot, going through the motions. Being asleep is doing what you've been told and trained to do by the dominant culture. Being asleep is "being nice" to the detriment of ourselves. Being asleep is saying *yes* to the demands and needs of others, but *no* to your own inner voice.

Being asleep is relinquishing authority over our own inner voice and inner truth and responding to others in a way that pleases them and meets their needs while judging ourselves harshly if we don't.

In the fairy tale, Sleeping Beauty had no alternative but to sleep and wait for the kiss of resurrection. But, today, in real life, women *do* have an alternative. Yet, so many of us do not see it. We perpetuate this sleep state by identifying with the powerless Sleeping Beauty because we've been taught that it's romantic and loving and we so desperately want to believe that that is true. But it's not romance and it's not love. It's powerlessness. Would a woman consciously choose powerlessness?

Lynn

Lynn's awakening came when she stopped giving her power away to gain acceptance and security. She learned to turn instead, to Spirit as her source of support and guidance.

Lynn

The highest level of creativity consists in being, not doing. When the being is intense enough, when the words are spoken enough, when the thoughts are thought enough, the doing will automatically follow.
—Marianne Williamson

I was asleep most of my life up until about five years ago. Life was very difficult. I had a lot of depression. I was really living my life by other people's roles and expectations. I was trying to be who everyone else wanted me to be. So, I was completely lost and depressed. Happiness was when I felt like I was meeting everyone's expectations. You can imagine how hard that is to orchestrate. All my energy was going into that, none into finding out who I was.

I was not aware that there was another reality. I thought that this was *it*. I remember asking God to please help me because this existence was just way too difficult. It became more and more apparent as I got older, and as my responsibilities as an adult increased, such as getting married, owning a home, having children.

I was pretty good at handling a lot, but we all have our breaking point, and when I had my fourth child, my last child, that was my breaking point. My plate was way too full, and I could no longer keep going. I couldn't keep up the masquerade. Looking back, my soul knew and my soul started to say, *it's time.*

I had a husband who was completely unsupportive and critical. I was able to get through most of the day with my children, but the worst part of the day was when my husband was going to come home and I would just feel my mood grow darker and the depression grew deeper starting around four o'clock. It happened pretty much every day. When he was home, that was when I was at my lowest. I look back and think how symbolic that was in terms of being asleep.

I had no identity as a child. I was searching for my identity through others. I attracted him into my life and he represented to me the person who was supposed to give me my identity.

My wake up came in like a tsunami. I met a person who triggered something in me that made me feel like I was something special just based on who I was and not what somebody else wanted me to be. That's what started it. I had thought about leaving my husband on and off for years, even when we were just dating, because the relationship was always rocky. I finally decided to do it. That started a chain of events that led to the complete destruction of my life.

Once it was destroyed, then I had to rebuild. Not only my life, but rebuild who I *was* because I certainly didn't know who I was. That's when the process started. I quickly started pulling in new resources. I began opening up to Spirit, knowing there was a higher power, because at that point I had nothing else. I had to have something because it was too painful. I drew teachers into my life, many teachers. The ones I needed at the time. They were my support. I started to read to find out what was happening to me and to learn more about what I was feeling in this early stage of awakening. It wasn't waking up and feeling all these beautiful things. It was difficult. But there was something there that I was able to grab onto, like treading water in the middle of the ocean and someone throws you a flotation device. It's not a whole lot, but it's something, and it's what's keeping you alive. There have been periods when I'm on a plateau, but I'm not going back and I haven't lost anything.

I stayed on my path of awakening with the help of Spirit and the help of people in my life; with my own search for meaning; knowing there was another reality; knowing there was a higher purpose at work. The mortal mind has limitations and Spirit is infinite. I began to feel the powerfulness of that. I felt a certain sense of security and safety knowing that if I focused on that, I felt much more at peace. I stopped pushing my own agenda.

I had one foot in the physical world and one foot in the spiritual world. Even now, when I'm struggling with situations, I keep reminding myself it's in the hands of God. I can't tell you how much more peaceful I feel. I feel like I don't have to carry the burden. I can let Spirit take over. Spirit is a hell of a lot more creative than I am.

I learned how to surrender, and I think that's what we're supposed to realize. That's where I experience miracles and synchronicities, and a flow. Once you've begun to wake up, and you live it at a higher state of consciousness, there's just no question about not going back.

One of the things I learned early on was not giving away my power. To rely on other people meant giving away my power. That was one thing I didn't want to do anymore. I also realized that I didn't have to do it on my own, I had help from Spirit, and I knew that I was meant to walk hand-in-hand with Spirit. People can disappoint you, but I'm never disappointed by Spirit. I've grown to realize that my agenda can be very limited, based on whatever my ego wants at the moment. I have to let go of my agenda and open up to what Spirit is offering.

Looking for the answer outside of myself was giving away my power and empowering others instead of empowering myself. I got tired of relying on the opinion of others I realized that was giving them power and feeding their egos, and then that gave me another whole set of problems to deal with. It made me feel depleted. I felt disempowered. That's how I operated for so much of my life. I started changing that. It was a sudden change. I went within to look for the answers.

I also had to limit who I can share with. I chose to share with those I know don't live mainly by their ego, those who are at a higher consciousness because then it can be more soul-to-soul.

Waking up is pretty amazing. It's energizing. It's joyful. It's absolutely incredible. And what's neat is it's not based on the external world. It's based on what I feel internally, and on my connection that I built with Source.

The ultimate gift for me is offering my children the wisdom, understanding, support, and guidance to help them through their difficulties. I became a teacher for them by example.

I sustain my momentum through taking care of my body, exercise, meditation, and moments where I'm alone and can have uninterrupted time where I can think. I spend time doing things I enjoy. I spend time with people I enjoy. I take the time to laugh and just have fun. Women are so good at taking care of others and completely neglecting themselves. They pride themselves on doing that because they've been taught that's what they're supposed to do.

1) Lynn's sleep state was the classic example of using all of her energy to meet the needs of others with nothing left for herself? How is this like your life? How do you carve out time and space for yourself?

2) Lynn states once her life was destroyed she had to rebuild it. When in your life did it feel like the end but it was really the beginning of a new life?

3) Lynn speaks about the importance of not giving away her power. In what ways do you give your power away?

Waking Up as an Act of Courage

The universe will reward you for taking risks on its behalf.
—Shakti Gaiwain

Many women see marriage and family as a safe haven from the need to perform in the outside world, a world they don't feel equipped to participate in fully. Girls and women judge themselves so harshly and spend so much energy attempting to perform to the increasingly unrealistic expectations of others that women's true selves lie dormant, unexplored and unexpressed. It's no wonder that so many feel ill-equipped to add more expectations—those of a demanding workplace—to the list.

Our ability to succeed in the outside world, however, really comes from our creativity, desires, and connection with ourselves. And those women who have not made those connections, those crucial steps in awakening, will, indeed fear venturing beyond focusing on appearance and pleasing a man.

In order for women to wake up, they need to find ways to redirect their energies from their own tyrannical inner critic and fear of others, and create a pathway to their inner Self through consistent time and attention.

Wow

Learned Helplessness

> If you just set out to be liked, you would be
> prepared to compromise on anything at
> any time, and you would achieve nothing.
> —Margaret Thatcher

So many women, especially if they've experienced childhood emotional or physical trauma, can't assert themselves and access their own sense of power. The concept of "learned helplessness" is at the core of this dilemma.

So many women who are aware of how powerless they feel in the world blame themselves for it. Blaming the victim is a classic control strategy used by a dominant culture or person. It never occurs to these women that this behavior and their perception of being powerless and ineffective in the world is something they've been *taught*.

Realizing this can be enormously liberating. No longer will you see your experience of powerlessness as a character defect, something you've created out of your own inadequacy. You will, instead, see it for what it really is—*learned helplessness*, the natural outcome of being bullied, tyrannized, and abused.

A friend who has worked for decades with batterers prefers the term *enforced helplessness* because it puts the responsibility on the perpetrator, where it belongs. This raises the question: *Is our power taken from us, or do we give it away under pressure to do so?* Which, then, raises another question: *What happens to the women who refuse to relinquish their power?*

Here are the answers:

Some women have their power taken from them.

Some women give their power away under pressure to do so.

All women who refuse to relinquish their power—whether they have role models to learn from and support systems that encourage them or not—still face the challenge of defending their right to be awake in the face of a patriarchal culture that is *not* happy with them.

When you are awake, connected to Self, and engaged in self-referral, the people and institutions with a vested interest in your being powerless and asleep will *not* be happy. That's *not* your problem. It's *theirs*.

The Inner World of Power

> I believe the lasting revolution comes from deep changes
> within ourselves, which influences our collective lives.
> —Anais Nin

When women are asleep, they are powerless and characterized by the Sleeping Beauty metaphor in which they are under a spell and living harmful, disempowering illusions and fantasy instead of reality.

When women are asleep, they are dependent and controlled, limited to assigned roles, often playing the victim role, fearful, desperate for love, living on autopilot, in the dark about what they want, and trapped in the cycle of expectations about pleasing others.

Women go to sleep—lose their power—through learned or enforced helplessness, playing assigned powerless roles, giving in to fear and intimidation, allowing themselves to become distracted, and allowing their powerlessness and all of its aspects to continue throughout their lives by repeating patterns.

But, when women are *awake*, they acknowledge and exercise their power and live from the inside out, not from the outside in. They know what they want, ask for it or provide it for themselves. They feel free to make choices. They love and nurture not just others, but also themselves. They stop waiting. They are able to connect with others as peers without being controlled or controlling others out of fear.

All of this is possible because the woman awake understands her Core Essence Self and has a healthy relationship to her Self as her center, source, and guide.

Women wake up—access, claim, and demonstrate their power and authority over their own lives—gradually or when they hear a wake-up call. They wake up against inner and outer resistance. They wake up by extending their nurturing to themselves. And by learning from others who have made the journey from asleep to awake. They wake up when they stop waiting and turn to the Self.

Ann

Ann's awakening was bolstered by
a strong foundation of honesty and
strength, and the willpower to hold her
intention to fulfill her purpose.

Ann

The older I get the greater power I seem to
have to help the world. I am like a snowball—
the farther I am rolled the more I gain.
—Susan B. Anthony

When you're young, you're real close to Spirit and you have the
Light with you. The first 15 years, I was really in my flow, and I
had that energy going. I look back at that time and I felt like I
was awake. In my teenage years, during the 1950s, the choices
for women because of the society's idea about women's roles,
meant that we were either mothers, wives, secretaries, teachers
or nurses. So, I went off to college and got married and did all
the dutiful things that I was supposed to do according to society.
And I fell asleep. I got out of touch with that raw spirit and natural energy of my first 15 years and went to sleep for 20 years until
the awakening came in 1970-1971 when I was about 35.

During those first 15 years, I was very athletic, very energetic. My parents weren't terribly supportive, but they weren't
inhibiting, either. And there was no violence in my family. I was
really free to develop. I recall one of my mother's standard lines
was, "Go out and play." Go out and play and you learn to be self-
sufficient, independent, to take care of yourself and solve your
own problems. So, I had that grounding in me.

But, then I closed down during the next 20 years for a number of reasons. One of them was that I was denying my own sexuality, which I had to do in the 1950s and 1960s. In order to be aware of another reality, I had to start owning these forces within me that I had buried and repressed.

When my kids were in grade school they came home for lunch, so I had these periods of time—two four-hour blocks in the morning and the afternoon that were totally mine to do with what I wanted. I started doing all the things that suburban white women do. I played in a golf league, went swimming at the Y, took a pottery class. It was depressing. We had a beautiful home on an acre and a half, and I remember standing in my kitchen looking out at the woods behind us and thinking, "Is this all there is? Is that what my life is going to be for the rest of my life?" I felt that something was *definitely* missing.

Then my father died. He'd been a very strong role model. He was a writer, he was very creative. He wrote books. He was a newspaper man. He was very enjoyable, fun, and loving, and a lot of my personality is similar to his. So, when he died, that was a pivotal event for me. It jarred me and I went into three years of therapy.

Also, during that time, there were about 20 of us who didn't like the way the local government was going. I was asked to participate in this campaign, and we ended up taking over the mayor's seat, the president of the council, and six out of seven council seats. Because of my work in this, I was appointed the first woman to the planning commission in the city. I felt like I was contributing, having a meaningful impact, not just playing golf and washing dishes. And I thought, I've got more to me than just being a suburban housewife. So, I decided to go back to school and get my Masters and PhD in psychology. This was in the early '70s and I was in my late 30s and early 40s.

I was in school with women who were in their 20s. They were very activist, and said, "What do you mean you're a house-wife?" That was the period of time when being a housewife was a no-no.

I was asked to speak at a conference. Women were being given an opportunity to really be themselves. That was a profound wake-up. My husband wondered, "Well, what's wrong with being a housewife?" And he said, "You're never here."

Shortly thereafter I got a divorce. That was the symbolism of moving away from that other reality of being a wife and the bounds of society. That was the last vestige because the guy I was married to was totally white male and patriarchal. Once I got a divorce, I was free. I could be whatever I wanted to be. Once I became free, I started developing a relationship with a woman and that opened up all this buried sexuality that I had totally denied and that society did not support. This was in the '90s, and it still wasn't very open. There wasn't gay pride.

So, first I got a divorce. Then, I owned my own sexuality. And the third thing was opening to Spirit. I began to explore mind, body, spirit. I went to some spiritual workshops. That supported and helped me sustain this growth.

I was becoming more and more capable of taking care of myself. I also had to take care of my kids, too. Right after my divorce, there was this horrible series of events with the kids, but we got through all of that. I just kept feeling it was going to be okay. I was going to survive. At that point, I was a survivor. I got a job, and from then there was just no stopping me. I was on the path.

I was getting promoted, and I thought that if others believed in what I was offering, then I must have something to offer. I looked inside and asked, "What is this that I have to offer inside of me?" I also took an 18-month organization and systems development program that taught me a lot about myself and how to handle myself in a variety of situations. That internal exploration had me examine my core values and beliefs. In my career I was getting a lot of respect and recognition. So, I got that external validation.

I felt comfortable with my own power. What a contrast. When I was married I was asking, "Is that all there is?" I had no power; no sense of myself as a competent, independent woman, and now I had this sense of my own power. I was a capable, competent, independent woman who did not need a man in order to make my life fulfilling.

Now, I feel connected to Spirit. I'm on course. It's very calming and peaceful when I'm in the flow and it just goes. It feels natural. How powerful can you be other than being in touch with the Source and be part of that?

I'm not even the same person, any more. At my 25th high school reunion 10 of the 12 of us who ran around together showed up, and it was amazing. Five of the women were still married. They were wives, did a lot of cooking, were members of their churches and PTA, and one of them had just become a grandmother. This was 1974, and they were still very much into the 1950's wife and mother socialization, playing tennis and golf. The other five of us were different: I had just completed my PhD and was working, one woman had just been appointed the very first female deacon of her denomination in her state, another woman was the warden at a big state prison, another woman was very successful in sales, and the other woman had bought some land out West and started an organic business. Here were five of us in the old life and five who had broken out into this new life. Five of us awakened. Five of us didn't.

I nurture my relationship with myself by not trying to. It sounds contradictory, but the way you nurture it is to let it grow and develop naturally. Be aware of and stay in the flow. It's like going back to when I was a kid again totally in touch with my body and mind, but now I am aware of Spirit.

1) Ann states that she felt awake until she was about 15 years old. How awake were you as a child? What was it like?

2) Ann went to sleep to function within the culture she lived in. In what ways have you put yourself to sleep to fit in?

3) Ann learned to be comfortable with her own power. In what ways are you comfortable with your own power and in what ways do you deny it?

Internal Excavation

What we do not make conscience emerges later as fate.
—C. C. Jung

By turning inward and learning their inner landscapes, the awakening woman learns to identify negative noise, and to clear blocks and debris including the false Self, defenses, and old wounds. Women wake up by finding the true Self and making the Self the source of choice, thereby changing their relationship to the Self for the better.

As a therapist, I see my role as assisting people in learning to explore their inner life and inner world. That's where the Core Essence Self lives. Thoughts, especially conscious thoughts, are literally only the tip of the inner world's iceberg. That tip on the surface is the conscious mind. Just as 75% of the iceberg is below the surface of the water, our unconscious world is at least 75% of our inner world.

This is the world of dreams, a direct avenue from the subconscious. This is the world of energy centers, intuition, unhealed wounds, stored traumas, fantasies, wishes, values, drives, impulses, buried feelings, and memories.

This is the world of denied aspects of the Self. It's where we tell ourselves ridiculous things like: "Good people are never angry, so I'm always polite," and "People won't like me if they think I'm lazy, so I'd better keep busy," and "I know my husband's mean to me, but I'm afraid to be alone."

In this submerged, below-the-tip-of-the-iceberg part of our inner world, we keep those parts of ourselves that we even hide from ourselves because they don't fit in with how we've been trained to think we should be. We have so much there and usually so little awareness of it. All of this blocks our awareness of who we *really* are, our Core Essence Self, our true Self.

On my desk in my office, I keep a quote by Virginia Satir that reads: "Make the abstract concrete, the implicit explicit, the hidden obvious, the covert overt." This describes exploring, navigating and excavating one's inner world. It's a therapeutic process at the core of every woman's ability to awaken and remain awake.

We are learning through quantum physics what metaphysics has been teaching for years: that the outer is simply a manifestation of the inner, and that *we* are the *cause* and the *material world* is the *effect*. It's as if we are the dreamer and the world is our dream. This is how we create our own reality. This is how we access our enormous power.

Defenses are the protective outer shell that covers the unconscious part of our inner world. All of us develop defenses as we adapt to the outside world. In order to become socialized, we develop a defensive structure to protect us from feelings, impulses, and wishes that interfere with this adaptation process. Uncovering what lies below these defenses is difficult to do alone or with friends. The defensive structure was formed in the first place because it felt like a life and death necessity, so the healthiest way to do this uncovering is in therapy within a strong, emotionally safe therapeutic relationship.

As you do this internal excavation work, energy that has been used to maintain the defensive structure is freed up to be used in engaging more fully in life. The defensive structure was established for good reason and dismantling it is scary, so surrounding yourself with supportive like-minded people is crucial when you do this internal work. Through this internal exploration, you discover more and more of your Core Essence Self, and you find that you have wisdom and strength within you that had also been covered by the debris of forgotten hurt and fears.

The more in touch you are with your Core Essence Self, the more awake you will be. And the more and more access you will have to the truth and to your center of love. When you connect to your Core Essence Self, you will be able to see from the inside out and live from the awareness that everything that counts *originates* on the inside.

The experience of discovering what lies below your defenses is much like the phoenix rising from the ashes. The outer False Self—which plays such a big role in every day life and includes our judgments, attachments, emotions, personality, addictions, beliefs, ego, will, attention to distractions, and so much more— is burned away by the use of deep, powerful self-awareness, and the true Self is given free rein to express itself in the world, from the center of your being. The world then becomes the stage on which you can play and express yourself. As you move into this way of being in the world, the Self as the *Source* is the energy pattern from which you live. You will live from the *soul* instead of from the False Self that was constructed in response to the material world. You will live from your true *identity*. Your identity is who you *really* are beneath the responses, reactions, and attachments to the material world.

The phrase "we are not human beings having a spiritual experience, but spiritual beings having a human experience," has become almost cliché, but it's true. If we believe what spiritual teachings tell us, we come from the divine and will return to the divine. The part that came and will return is our *identity*, often called the soul or spirit, which is separate from our *humanity* that resides in the world of form.

We are here to "bring Spirit into matter," to infuse the world of form with the essence of our true identity, to create heaven on earth, to let it be on earth as it is in heaven. Remembering who we are, *our* true *identity*, may be the most *crucial* task of our human existence, and is, literally, the *act* of waking up.

Sura

Sura's awakening came when she
released herself from the bondage of the
purely material, a value system so prized
by Western culture and so inherently
damaging to people and the planet.

Sura

Life engenders life. Energy creates energy.
It is by spending oneself that one becomes rich.
—Sarah Bernhardt

I remember a time in early 2000 when I was working on Wall Street in money management that I felt very disconnected. Most times, I felt jaded and unemotional. The way I would describe that experience is feeling really far from God. My value system was based on what was on the outside: how well I was doing in my career, how much money I made, the kind of relationships that I had. I felt like there was a black cloud following me everywhere, because everything I did never seemed to work out. Before that period, I felt engaged and lucky most times. Then I found myself in this place where I couldn't even believe in God or a larger life force anymore. I felt really shut down. That's when I felt the most asleep.

I was unaware of another reality. However, I always had some interest in religious and spiritual matters. I noticed that the happiest people seemed to have some kind of spiritual or religious practice.

I was at the top of my game working on Wall Street in New York. I had worked very hard, for two years straight without taking a break, so I'd planned a vacation to Southeast Asia. I made arrangements with my company to travel for four weeks. Before that time I'd started learning about Zen Buddhism, and meditation. These interests prompted me to go to Asia.

Shortly before my departure, the tsunami of 2004 struck, and I missed the tsunami by three days. The next morning, I read on the front page of the *NY Times*, that the resort I was to stay on had been completely wiped out. No one survived. I considered it a very close call. So, my wake-up call was the tsunami.

Something shifted in me. I thought to myself, "This is a second chance. I could have died." It was then that I was confronted with another reality. I cancelled the entire trip to Asia and booked a last-minute trip to Costa Rica.

In Costa Rica, I did everything I enjoyed. I engaged myself in life and took risks. I went whitewater rafting in the rainforest in class 4 rapids. Partway through our rafting journey, the river guides invited us to jump out in the middle of the canyons into the water. As soon as I jumped out into water, I started screaming. I couldn't contain myself. I felt so happy. It was a real happiness, which I hadn't felt in years. It was as if something awakened in me. In that moment, I realized, I can change my reality whenever I want. If I want "this," "to be in the rain forest," I can have it. I have the power to choose and create my reality. That very same week, some very synchronistic events happened—events that I considered to be a major sign from God. It was these events that led me to believe that I should study yoga at one particular place in Nosara, Costa Rica.

Around the time that I came back from my trip, my firm had promoted me to partnership level. It was a really heavy decision for me, one that I struggled and thought about for a while. It took all the courage I had to take a leap of faith and follow my inner calling to study yoga. My biggest support came from my mom, who encouraged me to follow my heart. What unfolded thereafter was a life transforming experience for me.

When I returned from Costa Rica, I decided to take a year off and take a spiritual pilgrimage around the world. I spent most of my time in India. There were times when it felt very chaotic, confusing and scary because I was traveling alone, and I wasn't sure what I was doing some of the time. Then I started to notice patterns. I noticed that if I just let go into what was happening, and stayed present with each moment, I knew what was coming out on the other side.

I noticed that there were times I would go into periods of darkness and confusion, depression; if I allowed myself to experience it fully and let go of my own resistance, those periods would be followed by a period of lightness and clarity. I always trusted in this process of growth and allowance. Allowing life to unfold without needing to know or control things. I knew that just because I was feeling low at certain points, those periods weren't always going to stay with me. I learned to let go of my own resistance and just let things happen. It was part of the process for me to experience the strength of my own faith and trust. So in that sense, I never felt that I went back "to sleep." I feel like I've seen too much to go back. I could not live in the same way as I did before.

I stayed on my path of awakening by creating self-discipline through yoga and meditation. During the time I traveled, I was dedicated to the process of sitting in stillness. What has kept me going is a vision and feeling of a mission. I feel I'm here for a Greater Purpose and to serve in a way that is fully empowering as a woman. I trust that everything around me, including all of my experiences and interactions, supports my inner growth and evolution. I believe this is true for all of us.

I began noticing that while I was sitting in my meditations. I started to receive insights and answers that were completely not my own, that I wouldn't have been able to think of on my own. When I could get still enough to just be okay without having to push or pull anything around, I could enter a neutral state and open my perceptual awareness. That was when I felt that I was a tiny little ant looking down at these ant hills at millions of other little ants, and we're all trying to make these decisions about what kind of clothes to wear and what kind of job to have. At the end of the day, it was as if we were all these tiny little ants.

As I'm waking up it feels like liberation and freedom. It's empowering to be able to choose from a place of love versus fear. There's more depth and so much more learning. I feel more engaged in the wonder and mystery of life. It's amazing to be able to see the extraordinary miracles in ordinary moments. Before, I felt like I was living only a portion of myself. I was only 20% of who I really was in my everyday interactions and exchanges with people. Now I feel the fullness, the embodiment of myself. I'm less shy about bringing it all to the table—the good, the bad, everything. I feel okay with offering all of myself to others without the need to hide or look good. I listen deeply. I listen to what I need and what would serve me. Ultimately, I know that what serves me serves the greatest good.

1) Sura describes her wake up call as the tsunami. Lynn writes her wake up call came like a tsunami. Have there been any tsunamis in your life? How did you change?

2) Sura states what keeps her going is a feeling that she has a Greater Purpose and that is true for all of us. If you knew what your Greater Purpose was what might it be?

3) Sura speaks about being more engaged in life as demonstration of her awakening process. When do you feel the most engaged in life? In what ways are you more disengaged?

Trusting the Self

> If I have lost confidence in myself.
> I have the universe against me.
> —Ralph Waldo Emerson

What does it mean to trust the Self? Self-trust is holding one's own counsel. It's Self-referral. It's being Self-affirmed. Self-trust means honoring the Self, your soul, as the central figure in your life. It's paying attention to your feelings, which are the clearest barometer of your internal environment, your internal truth. If I say I'm tired, I'm tired!

It's listening to that still, small voice within that comes from the Self, "the brain in the belly" which we sometimes call the gut, the voice on the inside, not the endless banter of things to do, and past and future preoccupations.

When you trust the Self, you listen to the information that comes from within, which you can do when you discount the outside information that interferes with Self-trust. Self-questioning and Self-criticism only undermine Self-trust. Self-trust requires unconditional love, of course—unconditional love for the Self.

We're required to trust so much early on in life. When we're young, if our parents are worthy of our trust, it works well. If they support you in trusting yourself, it's a wonderful thing. When we go to school, have babysitters, interact with anyone, we have issues of trust.

The educational system today unfortunately focuses almost exclusively on teaching children how to score well on tests. Recess, the arts, and other vehicles of self-expression have been eliminated in the service of preparing children for standardized tests. Education requires children not only to conform by quieting their own inner voices and inner guidance, but also to invest their precious life force into performance on standardized tests that merely meet the ego needs and monetary success of the school system. Many forces in our culture contribute to our falling asleep. The educational system that consumes the most hours of childhood works against remaining awake and true to the Self.

As adults, we go to work and are required to follow the rules of someone we may or may not trust. The capacity to remain loyal to your Self is significantly challenged as you move out into the world, which only wants to control you, so you have to remain true to yourself while being immersed in the socialization process. No one is exempt from the world's assault on the Self. How do we return to Self-trust and awaken after being immersed in this enormous socialization process?

It's a three-step process:

 1) First, remember that there *is* a Self.

 2) Listen to your *feelings*. That's the most direct avenue in returning to the Self because feelings originate on the inside. They may be a reaction to something on the outside, but the feelings themselves originate on the inside. The socialization process is

a layering on the Self of the rules and expectations of the larger culture. This energy flows from the outside in. But, your feelings are a *direct* expression from the Self, of what originates on the *inside*. This energy flows from the inside out. Listening to the Self is listening to the *voice* that comes from the *inside* out, *not* the conditioned voice that's been taught, but the voice that is pure, clear, and original.

3) Have a relationship with the Self in an environment of alert cu-riosity. Be like the cat who sits alert outside a mouse hole, curious about what's going to peek its head out. Alert attention and acute interest in whatever surfaces is a crucial piece of trusting the Self. When the information or awareness surfaces, refrain from any programmed response that disconnects or diminishes it.

Self-trust grows when you give yourself the quiet time to focus on your inner world and listen to what your Self is telling you. Having like-minded friends who do this, too, and support your Self-trust, can make all the difference in the world.

Creativity as Expression of the Self

> Why should we all use our creative power...? Because
> there is nothing that makes people so generous, joyful,
> lovely, bold, and compassionate, so indifferent to
> fighting and the accumulation of objects and money.
> —Brenda Ueland

Creativity is an expression of the Self. When you live from the inside out, you know and speak your truth, you act from inner prompts, and you will literally *create* your life from your own guidance.

Using your creative energies means living from the inside out rather than seeking direction from the outside in. You function from your creative center, rather than perform according to the demands of the outside world, by first remembering that "where your attention goes, your energy flows."

Turn inward to your Self and ask, "What do I *want* to do?" Want is a feeling that comes from the Self. Desire originates internally, which always makes it in alignment with who you are at your deepest level. This want is an expression of what you want to *create*, not material objects you want to accumulate—that is from the ego. The want from the Self is a *creative* expression from the inside, while the want from the ego is about *getting* something from the outside. The want from the Self is a desire to *add* something to the world. The want from the ego is a desire to fill a bottomless pit of *acquisition*.

Once you become clear about your desire for creative expression, begin it. You don't have to know where you're going with it long-term. Just start focusing on it and pulling energy into it. Also look around your life and see where you're plugging your creative energies into your daily activities. Then, create a supportive structure for your *new* creative energies. You will find that the energy will grow, and you'll manifest new opportunities for creative expression because when you create, you are literally plugging into an energy field.

It's hard to maintain clear channels to your creativity, your authentic Self, without resolving emotional blocks as they show themselves, so remember to process through old residue. And, don't forget to carve out a space in your life for this creative expression.

A woman awake lives from her creative Self, so creativity is one of the most powerful energies in waking up and staying awake. The "fire in the belly" is passion and creativity. Feed your creative fires. Feed them the connection and attention to the inner Self—first, the moment of contact, and then the quiet present moment filled with alertness to the spark of inspiration. A spark ignites, then a fire burns, bringing alertness, attention, and trust. Follow it. Trust yourself, and allow the process to unfold. Don't worry about where it's going. Go for the ride. Be true to your inner voices, inner visions and other forms of inspiration that fuel the entire process.

Writing it Down

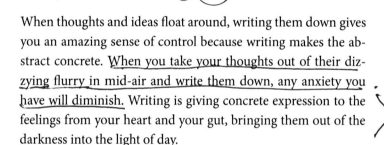

You sort of start thinking anything is
possible if you've got enough nerve.
—J. K. Rowling

When thoughts and ideas float around, writing them down gives you an amazing sense of control because writing makes the abstract concrete. When you take your thoughts out of their dizzying flurry in mid-air and write them down, any anxiety you have will diminish. Writing is giving concrete expression to the feelings from your heart and your gut, bringing them out of the darkness into the light of day.

Writing gives you a way to communicate with yourself. If you're overwhelmed by thoughts, feelings, tasks, or anything else, you can write them down and the burdensome, overwhelming sensation will be released.

It doesn't matter whether you think your writing is good or not. This isn't about being a wonderful writer or an astute literary critic. This is about Self-expression. Write it all out. Keep it or throw it away, it's up to you. Show it to someone or keep it private, it's up to you. Just get it *out* of you and in writing. It will feel like you're exhaling the most powerful breath of relief. Let it all out.

Remember that writing is just talking out loud on paper (or, these days, perhaps on a computer screen). If you write the way you speak, you'll do just fine. Don't worry about grammar, it'll come out fine if you write the way you hear it in your head and say it out loud.

Writing helps you focus and bring order to your floating thoughts, and it helps you clarify them, delve into what they mean and how you feel about them. Writing shows you what's on your mind.

You may be surprised at just how much comes out of you when you begin to write it down. And how much you didn't consciously realize was there waiting to get your attention, waiting to surface. When you write honestly, it's almost impossible to be asleep. The act of writing is an awake act.

Writing helps clear your internal clutter. The Self can't live amongst the clutter, the clutter in your mind or in your physical environment. So, creating inner and outer space helps you to perceive the Self and communicate with it. Quiet space. Quiet space with no distractions.

clutter clutter clearing clutter

Catherine
Catherine's awakening shows us what
happens when you look through the
eyes of Spirit and never go back.

Catherine

The only event in the history of our species that compares with this one is genesis. And this is a new kind of genesis, that genesis of our species into conscience awareness.
—Gary Zukav

My earliest memories of when I was asleep was when I was very young, and certainly wouldn't have labeled things spiritual. When I was a pre-teen, I'd go to church with my family, but something just didn't seem right about it. I knew there was something more to this whole spirituality question, and I knew for me the way toward it wasn't going to be through religion because organized religion didn't fit with me. Even as a really young child, when we'd be singing hymns I'd be changing the words to them and singing them. I would just say, "Well, I think it's really this way," or "I think it's really that way," or "I don't believe that God is male," so I'd change the gender in the hymn. And I was really little. Adults would turn around in the row in front of me and say, "*What* is she singing?" I didn't know why I was doing that, but I just had this really deep feeling that there were some improvements to be made.

I had this deep feeling that there was something more than just going to church on Sunday, saying grace, and things like that, that there was something out there. I had no idea what it was yet. It felt uncomfortable. There were answers I didn't have. The world didn't make sense yet. I knew there was something there that I had to uncover or dig deep to find, but I had no idea how that was supposed to happen.

I'd say that I was still basically asleep even when I'd graduated from college, although I do remember one epiphany moment when I was in college. I was very sad that my parents were getting divorced, but one day I was looking out the window, and I looked up at the building across from me and noticed how unbelievably intricate and ornate the top of that building was. It had copper that had turned that beautiful bluish green color, and these ornate shapes and filigree designs, and I thought, that is the most beautiful thing I've seen in a really, really, really long time.

It was a moment. I really think it was some kind of spiritual awakening. Although I was still asleep in terms of defining my own spirituality, it was a wake-up call. It was like God tapped me on the shoulder and said, "Look at things differently, look at the world around you differently, look at your life differently, look at the beauty that surrounds you. And start looking for the beauty around you."

The magnitude of what I felt in that moment was so enormous that it stayed with me the rest of my life. It pulled me right out of my depression. I'd looked at that building a hundred times before and it had never looked that way to me. Life didn't look the same after that.

As I continued on this path I was definitely aware that there was something I didn't know, and I felt like I was waiting for *something*. I didn't feel like I was waiting for *someone*. I just looked at it as if I was going to discover something someday by doing research, by investigating, or by having some kind of experience that gave me access to deeper wisdom and knowledge. I believed that I'd have an experience in spirituality at some point or a spiritual awakening of some kind, and that's how I'd find out about it. I didn't think I'd find out about it necessarily from other people. I thought it was something you had to experience directly in some manner.

I was interested, though, in finding people who I could learn things from who had had these kinds of experiences. I went through several stages where I nominated a person as my spiritual guide who I felt knew more than I did about spirituality and had some kind of wisdom or knowledge that I was looking for. I got burned many times by putting people up on that pedestal. I finally realized that I wasn't supposed to have somebody who was a teacher or mentor. Every time I did it and tried to make someone else's experience of spirituality more important than my own, or tried to live by their experience too much, it didn't work out. I'd pick people who had very large egos and it would always backfire.

So, I realized that I'd been right when I was little about my definition of spirituality—that it was going to be direct experience and not come from someone else. This is not to say that I don't learn from other people, because I do. I was just never meant to make any one person my be-all-end-all guide on this path. Every time I tried to do that, it would blow up in my face. I was so naïve. I thought spiritual people are all good people, and I'd join these groups and they'd end up being like a cult. There are a lot of dogmatic belief systems out there that people get very rigid about. It becomes too much like religion when that happens. So, now I just talk to a spiritual director whom I've talked to for years, and he doesn't impose anything on me. It has been so refreshing to have a person with that strength of character in my life. He consistently hasn't wanted to "over direct me" and yet he offers incredibly valuable information and wisdom. He's agendaless, except for wanting to be helpful.

My awakening process was gradual. When I'd just graduated from college, I got hit by a car. I could have died. A very elderly man in a large station wagon hit me on my left hip and I went over the hood and bounced back and then hit my head on the street. And there was a bus coming. The man driving the car had been looking at the bus and not me or where he was going.

Someone scooped me up and got me to the sidewalk and said, "Are you okay?" I said, "Yes." I'd hit the back of my head incredibly hard, and my face, on the front of the hood, and my left hip. I turned black and blue on the whole left side of my body, but I didn't break anything. This tall African American man got me to the sidewalk and then disappeared. It didn't seem normal. I think it was angelic presence of some kind because it just doesn't add up that he could just disappear like that. Also, the feeling of being moved to the sidewalk wasn't normal, either. I'd felt weightless.

That whole experience was a big wake-up call. I started getting involved in alternative medicine and ways to heal spiritually. I wanted to use that accident experience for the greater good. I read everything I could get my hands on that was spiritual, and all sorts of things on esoteric thoughts, and native belief systems. I have a little bit of Cherokee blood, so I'm interested in them as well. It was interesting to find the doors that it opened. I started reading Sylvia Brown's books, and they validated a lot of the experiences I'd been having. As a child, I grew up in a haunted house. A lot of my childhood I was very afraid because I could sense these energies around me but no one else in my family could. Sylvia Brown's writing about spirits that are caught in between made so much sense to me and I started to feel normal. I'd felt like such a freak being able to sense there was a presence. When you're a child you really can't explain that.

I maintain my momentum mostly through reading. It kept it all alive for me and kept me learning things and curious about things. Later, I realized I didn't necessarily need to read so much, that I could also experience it more directly myself. Luckily, I had a very dear friend who was also waking up around the same time.

Once I was on this path it didn't even occur to me that going back was even an option. I've always been about balance in my life. When I chose to go down this path, I didn't go down it as far as some of my fellow seekers did who reconfigured their entire life to be all about spirituality. I felt that my role was more to help people come to their own awakening. To do that I needed to be in the world and mix in normal everyday society and everyday people and not seclude myself and surround myself with 100% spiritual world people. I'm bringing spirituality into everyday life. I want to make this happen in the real world and change the real world because of it, and not have to go onto a secluded mountaintop or keep spirituality from regular life.

Somebody told me that our function as human beings is to bring Spirit into matter. My spiritual director talks about concentric circles, where your everyday material life is like a pie chart, with career, relationships, physical body, as pieces of the pie, but there's an outer circle of spirituality that surrounds all of it. So, you can't get away from spirituality because it's all part of spirituality. He says the danger is that people make spirituality *one* of those pieces of the pie. In my life, I bring spirituality into everything, into making hors d'oeuvres for a party, into helping someone up the stairs on the subway.

As I developed more I knew the power was definitely going

to come from some connection within, but at the beginning I thought my energizing quality was going to have to come by pulling it in from an outside Spirit. At first, I erroneously assumed that I had to go to some effort and/or be magnetic in some way to attract and pull Spirit to me, and that paradigm is exhausting. I figured out that it's not about *pulling* in Spirit, it's about *receiving* Spirit. It's about opening up to Spirit—it's already there. There's nothing you have to do to activate it or actively go out and grab it. Once I figured that out, I stopped the mad rush of trying and seeking under every rock for my spirituality. It was one of those ah-ha moments. I don't have to work hard to be a spiritual entity. I already *am* one. That revelation gave me much more energy in my spiritual life. Energy was available to me almost like having an internal battery pack that's always recharging instead of having to plug into something.

Now, I have much more patience with things that I want to change about my life, or things I want to have happen or be different. I have much more faith and less anxiety about my life, its course and direction. I had too much drive almost. I felt like I had to go out and *make* something happen in my life, and the same thing with my spirituality. I didn't know how to receive spirituality and spiritual connection. In the material world, I didn't understand how to receive events at their own unfolding pace. I didn't realize there's a grander plan. There are things you can do to help things along, to make the universe understand what your wishes are, but you don't need a fire hose to water the plants in your own garden of life, a watering can is just fine.

Life works when you're listening to the organic signs that are about which way to go and how to do something, and then putting your energy where it's most effective. I live in the city and whenever I'm outside I'm in constant contact with tons of people, and lots of times somebody needs help in some way. A tourist who's lost or someone needs help up the stairs, or someone's carrying something they can't quite manage. There are little things that I become aware of and I do little nice things for people. The small things are more important in my spirituality than the big things. That's where it's really at for me in terms of keeping things alive on a day-to-day basis. I do things for myself that keep my sense of Self intact. I feel like a huge yellow happy face on the subway in the morning. I almost feel out of place.

1) Catherine's awakening began as a spiritual experience. Have you had any spiritual experiences that changed how you saw the world?

2) Once Catherine began her waking up process she began looking for teachers outside herself. What has been the role of teachers in your awakening process?

3) Catherine believed there was an angelic presence that saved her from death. Have you had any experience that felt like angels intervened or appeared to you?

4) Catherine stated "Somebody told me our function as human beings is to bring Spirit into matter. What does that mean to you?

Embracing Nature and Reducing Negative Noise

Meet everyone and everything through
stillness rather than mental noise.
—Eckhart Tolle

The best way to reduce negative noise is to go out in nature.
Nature nourishes the Self, quiets the surface mind, helps you to
awaken and keeps you awake.

When I reflect on the deepest connections with my Self, it's
most often in connection with nature: listening to the water and
the birds chirping, feeling the breeze on my face, watching a butterfly or a bird.

Immersing yourself in nature creates a feeling of inner spaciousness.

Take a walk.

Turn off the cell phone and anything else you could plug into
your ear.

Make a space for the Self.

Slow down and vibrate in harmony with nature.

It's where you were born to live, after all. You're already wired
for it.

To wake up and stay awake, you must keep your vibration

high. There's nothing in the world that lowers vibration like negative noise. The most toxic form of negative noise is gossip. Gossip is talking with someone negatively about a third person who isn't present for the conversation. Contrary to popular belief, gossip is not an insignificant, harmless way to pass time and make conversation. It's a powerful misuse of energy. Gossip not only lowers your own vibration, it also transmits negative energy to the person you're gossiping about.

Television is another significant form of negative noise. The TV's sound pollution is disruptive to your energy, and it's impossible to listen to your inner voice when you're constantly glued to the television. The huge fluctuations in volume designed to attract your attention—like commercials that are louder than the programs they interrupt—are jarring to your psyche and your energy. So is the rapid-fire yelling of the car salesman in the obnoxious commercial, the onslaught of violence in so many of the shows, and the national and local news that entices you to watch by manipulating you into a chronic state of apprehension, worry and fear.

Computers are perhaps the most deceptively negative tools in our life today. Touted as time saving devices, they actually are the opposite, and end up enslaving us to them. The negative noise, energy drain, and physical and emotional stress caused by computers (as well as other "wired" devices such as i-pods, i-phones, etc.) is phenomenally damaging.

Incessant whining and complaining in a way that drains you also takes its toll as negative noise. Healthy venting is one thing, but self-destructive, stuck-in-the-mud, "oh, poor me" routines designed to keep you a victim wallowing in negativity isn't going to help you at all. It will keep you stuck and powerless.

Mindless small talk is less toxic, but guaranteed to put you to sleep, literally and spiritually. Have you ever noticed how restless, yet drained, it makes you feel when you'd prefer to have an interesting conversation but the other people around you seem incapable of anything but boring, mindless chatter, usually about material things?

You can also have negative noise in your head: the endless fears, anticipations, plans, and worries that demand your attention and prevent you from hearing the Self's voice.

So many of the distractions, energy-drainers, and elements of negative noise come in small increments that cumulatively take their toll on us. Maya Angelou talks about negative outside sources insidiously picking away like ducks pecking at us. A little piece here, a little piece there, and before you know it we've all been pecked to death by ducks.

We have free will and we can choose to limit our exposure to all forms of negative noise so that we can create the best space possible in which to hear the Self's voice. Having a strong relationship with that voice is vital to waking up and staying awake.

Debbie

Debbie's awakening shows us that
life is full of changes, surprises, and
synchronicity, but guidance will always
flow through you. If you listen to it,
you can ride the currents of life as a
spiritual voyage.

Debbie

> If you deny yourself access to the child within because
> you're too serious, you also block your connection to
> the divine light and your feminine self. Every creator
> who's any good uses their feminine side to create with…
> whether a scientist working on a hunch, a painter working
> on a interplay of colors, or a musician dealing with the
> juxtaposition of notes and chords.
>
> —Stuart Wilde

I can recall several times in my life where I truly thought I was living with clarity, only to be met with an "Aha" moment where I realized I had actually been on auto pilot for weeks or even months. I believe we go through waves of sleep and wakefulness. We live lives of continual challenge and reward; it is when we feel "on purpose" that we have the clarity of wakefulness.

I believe my adolescence was when I was most asleep, when I didn't recognize that I was primarily functioning outside of myself. The first truly powerful "awakening" I experienced was when I was 15 years old. I was depressed, my grades were falling, I was spinning out of control. I was only 15 and trying to figure out how to commit suicide without my parents feeling like it was their fault or that they did anything wrong. It was early afternoon; I was leaning against a tree atop a hill which over looked the elementary school I had attended. I drifted off and fell asleep while sorting out my fate. I woke nearly five hours later; it was getting dark and cold outside. My awakening literally happened when I woke up.

I had a new understanding. I realized that I had a very strong, healthy body and shouldn't just throw this life away. I decided that I could—and *should*—contribute. I decided I would join the Peace Corps, thinking that if I died saving *one* person who was meant to live to change the world, then *I* would have done my part to make the world a better place. It seemed to me to be a more honorable way to die. By shifting my perspective, I got myself out of that desperation. I brought my grades up, excelled in sports over the summer, and things kind of leveled out. I never ran away to join the Peace Corps. I began to contribute in ways I could; I realized I wanted to make a positive difference in the world by *living* honorably.

Earlier I wanted someone to save me, to show me my worth. After that literal wake-up call, my growth was gradual and I slowly started taking power back. I gravitated to people who seemed to have depth and stuck with people who had insight and shared their philosophies with me. I became a sponge for spiritual thought and practices.

We talk about our experiences as women, but so much happens when we're girls—in our adolescence. We may take our *own* story of "growing up" seriously, but years later as adults, when we talk to a teenage girl, we don't think of them as the powerful beings that they are. They have some incredible things going on in their lives. People are born as big souls in little bodies. Then we have to work our way through until the body is big enough that we can actually put into play some of these things that we came onto the planet to do. You come into the body as an infant and you're basically taking a vow of silence for two years. You can't speak—only observe. We have our childhood experiences to prepare us for the work we are meant to do in this lifetime.

My awakening was a transformation. It was the beginning of my seeing that I was not circumstantial. That I have a purpose. Killing myself would have been physically transforming; *not* killing myself was spiritually transforming. I learned that the ability to change my *perspective* is fairly simple, yet incredibly powerful. Someone who feels power-*less* is not seeing all of her options. Understanding that concept can turn anyone's life around.

Now, I try to see life as our playground instead of taking everything so seriously and personally. Everyone has their own story and their own filter that *everything* comes in and out of. Not everything that happens has something to do with *me*. I strengthened my awakening by my enthusiasm for learning new things, getting more information, meeting new fascinating people. It is a deepening. It is also maintained by my very strong innate need to be of service, to help people.

I know that I don't ever have to stay in an unhappy situation. There are always other options. My mom would say, "Always have a Plan B." This is a way of seeing that in any situation, there is typically more than one option. I never went completely back to sleep again.

There was a point that I realized I had to rescue myself. This goes back to when I recognized that I was taking my power back, and that everything that was making me feel healthy had come from my *own* initiation. I recognized how much power I really have in my own life, even though before that I felt that I had absolutely none. I let go of the rescue fantasy. Instead, I started to see potential. The potential of connection and collaboration

with other people, rather than someone rescuing me out of desperation.

When a woman's path or passion takes her outside of the
"tribal" agreement, she needs to leave the tribe. Often, she gets
kicked out of the "tribe," and that can be hurtful. She can leave
with grace, or feel dis-graced. She may feel isolated. That might
happen to women when they awaken. As a child and young
woman, I always did what I *thought* I was "supposed to do." I
was respectable in high school, I went to a Big Ten college and
finished in four years. All the goals that I had were so tribal. I
would have loved to have traveled overseas and studied overseas, but, that was not allowed. It was *not* part of the tribal agreement. When I turned 22, I packed my little car with my few
belongings and moved from Michigan to California against the
wishes of every single person in my "tribe," my family, most of
my friends. I had a lot of opposition from people. I didn't have
much support from anyone, mostly just fear. Only a couple of
people understood that it was what I needed to do, but it was
completely against the tribe.

A lot of times, women depend on the tribe, or someone in
the tribe, to rescue them. To see them for who they are and to
support them. They also know that if they do something the
tribe doesn't approve of, they'll be disowned by the only people
that they know "love" them. It all goes back to love and acceptance. You want love and acceptance, so if a woman's heart takes
her in a different direction, she'll often ignore her own wishes
and "go to sleep" because it's easier than having to face isolation
with no love or acceptance.

However, everyone needs to take responsibility for their
path. No one can see what's special in you until you recognize
it in yourself and allow it to show. So, instead of waiting to be

rescued, which is outward, a woman needs to go inward and take a look so that she can move forward and really develop that part of herself.

I often have to remind myself that the power lies on the inside. I also surround myself with people I love and trust who have no problem calling me on the carpet to remind me. When I am grounded and focused, there is a serenity knowing I have control over feeling full of my own energy. It's feeling comfortable where I am, wherever that may be.

Now, I enjoy every day so much now rather than having my happiness dependent on another person's opinion or completion of a goal on the horizon. I can now enjoy having the goal and having dreams and things I want to manifest, but the true pleasure is in every day of the process. I love the synchronicities which support my complete belief in miracles! The people who pop up out of the blue, the connections we make, the energy in it all. I think it was Anaïs Nin who said, "Every day is a mini-life." Those days add up. People are so focused on what they don't have or what they're working toward that they don't see the little victories and the beautiful little moments. Or the incredible souls they encounter every single day.

I find that an integral aspect of being awake is being in and savoring the moment. I tease friends who are resisting things which "pop up" which do not fit in their "Plan" that the Universe is "sashaying" them into a different direction. That they should pay attention and ask what the message might be vs. immediately deciding it is "wrong." I have a friend who talks about how she has the "Chef" archetype. It's about finding different "ingredients" in life and pulling them together and making something great.

Now, as I go through my days I try to check in with myself— take my emotional temperature, figure out if I feel "on track" with my heart path. I meet with people who are spiritually and energetically aware, who ask me the tough questions and support me through the process of answering honestly. I <u>exercise</u> and do things that will strengthen me and keep me healthy. It's how I nurture my soul in a lot of ways, appreciating beautiful scenery, the ocean, the miraculous parts of nature. I recognize how I contribute. We're so quick to see other people's beauty, strengths, and the things that make them special, but we hesitate to honor those things in ourselves. The truth is, if we can see something in them, there must be a part of us which embodies that quality, too.

1) Debbie's awakening came at her darkest hour when she was considering suicide. Have you ever had moments of surrender that turned out to be turning points?

2) Debbie speaks of the risk of being "kicked out of the tribe" if one follows their own path. In what ways do you silence yourself and adapt to avoid being "kicked out of the tribe?"

3) Debbie states "We're quick to see other people's strengths but we hesitate to honor these in ourselves. What are qualities you see in others that you might embody yourself?

Indra's Net

There is an endless net of threads through the universe…

At every crossing of the threads there is an individual.

And every individual is a crystal bead.

And every crystal bead reflects

Not only the light from every

Other crystal in the net

But also every other reflection

Through the entire universe.

—Rig Veda

Living Life Awake

Other people attempt to live their lives backward; they try
to have more things or more money, in order to do more of
what they want, so they will be happier. The way it actually
works is the reverse. You must first be who you really are,
then do what you need to do, in order to have what you want.
—Margaret Mead

<u>As each of us wakes up, we stand up by claiming our own power</u>,
we form a matrix of love and light by connecting with others
in compassion, empathy, and respect, and we heal the planet,
returning to the oneness that is at the core of all religions and
spiritual teachings.

Awakening begins with a wake-up call, a prompt for turning
inward and seeing oneself and the world differently. Throughout
the book you have met 11 women of all ages and all walks of life,
none of them famous, who have awakened and can show us the
way. These women are standing up and letting their light shine,
adding to the energy of a global matrix that is also folding in the
men and moving us to a new level of awakening on the planet.

The women's wake-up calls acted as catalysts for moving
from outer-focus and attachment to form, to inner-focus and
non-attachment. Each wake-up call achieved this in a different

way, but all served the purpose of signaling each woman to shift her trajectory from seeking on the outside to exploring and attending to her inside world, her Core Essence Self.

These role models have walked ahead and shown us the way.

We can join them.

Women who are awake polish their diamond inside "the Self" so that it can reflect the light. It reflects out into the world as a beacon of light that others can follow.

A Call to Action
Women *Waking*
the World

A Call to Action:
Women Waking the World

If ever the world sees a time when women shall come
together purely and simply for the benefit of mankind,
it will be a power such as the world has never known.
—Matthew Arnold

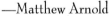

This book is literally *a call to action*: The time is now, and awakened women are leading the way in waking up the planet.

Because you have to wake yourself up before you can wake up the world; throughout the book we looked at the awakening process, as well as *why now?* and *why women?* and we met 11 women who show us the way.

Now, we'll look further at that effort to wake up the world—and hear from more women who have inspired ideas about how to do that—as we call you to action so that you can play your part in the Great Awakening.

Wisdom of the Elders

There's a river of birds in migration
A nation of women with wings
—A woman's spirituality round

In the Winter 2006-2007 issue of the magazine *Point of Light*, psychotherapist and writer Vikki Hanchin, LSW, called our attention to native prophecies that point to the significance of the few years leading up to 2012, which, as the end of the ancient Mayan calendar, signifies not the end of the world, but the transformation of the world for the better.

"Some of these prophesies say that now is the time for gathering and mobilizing women, because it is 'through the voices of women that the future will be ensured,'" Hanchin noted. "It is a Native American prophesy that, 'When the Grandmothers, speak, peace will return to the Earth, and the Earth will be healed.' Interestingly, in 2004, 'The Alliance of 13 Indigenous Grandmothers' from around the world, established their proclamation of concerns and commitments to help Mother Earth, and inspired hosts of similar wise-women gatherings across the country. There is indeed a growing public awareness that the choices humanity makes during the next few years may well determine whether life as we know it will be able to continue flourishing on this planet Earth."

In 2003, one year before the Grandmothers made their proclamation, the Elders of the Native American Tribe, Hopi Nation, People of Peace issued their message to the world:

A Message from the Hopi Elders

"We have been telling the people that this is the Eleventh Hour.

Now you must go back and tell the people that this is the Hour.

And there are things

To be considered.

Where are you living?

What are you doing?

What are your relationships?

Are you in the right relation?

Where is your water?

Know your garden.

It is time to speak your truth

Create your community.

Be good to each other.

And do not look outside yourself for the leader.

This could be a good time!

There is a river flowing

Now very fast.

It is so great and swift that there are those who will be afraid.

They will try to hold onto the shore.

They will feel they are being torn apart and they will suffer greatly.

Know the river has its destination. The elders say we must let go of the shore, and push off and into the river,

Keep our eyes open, and our head above the water.

See who is in there with you and Celebrate.

At this time in history, we are to take nothing personally.

Least of all ourselves.

For the moment that we do,

Our spiritual growth and journey comes to a halt.

The time of the lone wolf is over, Gather yourselves

Banish the word struggle from your attitude and your vocabulary

All that you do now must be done in a sacred manner

And in celebration.

We are the ones we've been waiting for."

—The Elders,
Hopi Nation, People of Peace
Oraibi, Arizona (2003)

Because We Say So

This is the most interesting time in human
history. This is the time when it's up to us to make
the difference as to whether we live or whether we die.
—Jean Houston

Interestingly, Gather the Women was also formed by women in their grandmother years. Elders, whether they are from native tribes or not, are answering the call from Mother Earth to lead the way. Women of *all* ages are answering this global call to action.

"We are remembering at last our forgotten powers, not only to physically procreate but to spiritually regenerate. We're going to change history: We're going to turn the *Titanic* around this time before it hits the iceberg; we're going to miraculously stop the insane, suicidal march now presided over by the governments of the world; and it's going to happen *because we say so,*" Marianne Williamson wrote in *The Age of Miracles.*

Because we say so…how many times have mothers said that to their children? It's the phrase a mother uses to signify her final word and to claim her final authority.

That authority is beautifully and powerfully rendered in the final glyph from the Mayan prophecies that show an image of the staff of power being handed over to a woman, the collective feminine at this predicted time of 2012.

Tend & Befriend

Women and Earth are inseparable.
The fate of one is the fate of the other.
—Thomas Perry

Research at UCLA in 1991 revealed that men and women respond differently to what they perceive as stress. Men react with the classic "fight or flight" response we've all heard about.

But, women's "bonding" hormone oxytocin is activated when women perceive stress, so a women's response is quite the opposite of a man's, and is described as "tend and befriend." Women take care of and connect. Awake women can expand this natural response to include the planet. This is how we save the world.

"As a mother bear protects her cubs, women will protect the earth," Jean Shinoda Bolen explained in *Urgent Message from Mother, Gather the Women Save the World.*

We Are the Ones
We've Been Waiting For

We men have had our turn and made a proper mess of things.
We need women to save us. Time is running out.
—Archbishop Desmond Tutu

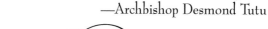

Jean Bolen, who states she sees herself as a messenger, further describes this unique point in time we find ourselves in her book, *Crones Don't Whine.*

"Of all the human beings, male and female, who have *ever* lived on planet Earth, we who are in the prime years of cronehood now were the first who, as a generation, have had the opportunity of being maternal women *and* achievers in the outer world. It has been possible for us to make choices and learn consequences, and integrate both feminine and masculine principles into our psyches. We could easily be a short-lived resource, a never-again historical fluke, if fundamentalist religions and the patriarchal attitude that they spawn have their way. Humanity is on a destructive course, one way or another, and life on this planet is endangered by male human beings with power. Time seems to be running out on *Homo sapiens.* Biologically, the continuation of the species has always been up to women.

Now I think that it is up to crones—women and the exceptional men who deserve the name—to bring forth the *sapiens* (which means *wise* in Latin) in time to insure the spiritual, psychological, and intellectual continuation of humanity."

Those Who Walk Ahead and Show Us the Way

> Our deepest fear is not that we are inadequate. Our deepest fear is that we are powerful beyond measure. It is our Light, not our darkness, that most frightens us.
> —Marianne Williamson

I interviewed many women for this book and asked them questions about their awakenings. I also asked each one how they saw the role of the collective feminine in the awakening of the planet. Each woman spoke from the diamond of her Core Essence Self. Each described her vision of the individual and collective feminine energy acting as a catalyst to usher in the awakening of the earth. These women were all intuitively aware of the urgency of this sacred mission to save Mother Earth and the innate qualities women bring.

The following is a sprinkling of diamonds from these awakening women.

When women are **supportive** and **loving** and **collaborative**, we're so **powerful**. Women underestimate their power, not just our positive power, but our negative power, too. We don't acknowledge our **anger**. We're trained to not feel it or not express it if we do feel it.

Each person plays a different role in **waking up** the planet. Each person's calling is important and individual. Each person has to find out what they're **good at** and what they **love**.

Lani

We're already playing that role by uniting together and forming spiritual connections. We don't realize it, but on an energy vibrational level we're creating a grid around the world. Women are the instruments in that. The more we connect with our conscious awareness, that energy creates a grid of protective energy around the earth. We're doing that so we can save earth. The more of us that light up, the more that grid is formed.

We're becoming **stronger**. We know we've got a better connection with our **spirit**. Our self-esteem for years has been low, but it's **rising**, and the more it rises, the more **confident** we are, then the more we create a stronger grid.

We move out of being the servant and we become an individual, and we become mothers to the planet because we are the nurturing souls. Females are the nurturers, and there are more women awakening in their later years than ever before now.

Sandy

It's happening all around the globe. Women are taking the initiative. More women are not allowing themselves to be defined by men. Women are just waking up all over the place and they're waking up on spiritual, relationship, and emotional levels rather than using their power in destructive ways. They're building community and synergy, attracting rather than repelling, pointing out similarities rather than differences. They are starting to get the money, now, too. We've made these inroads in such a profound way and there's no going back.

Along with this comes a responsibility to help, like the women of Darfur who are being raped, and with the horrific AIDS epidemic in Africa. If we're going to step up to the plate, then we're going to address these huge issues. I'm a citizen of the world, not just of the United States. That means what happens throughout the world impacts me. When you take on these

Ann

global issues, make sure you speak your truth and stay in your flow. Contribute your energy to the universal good. With women waking up, we're creating a critical mass.

As women become more empowered, I believe we'll see less separation in society. Hopefully, we'll have a more nurturing, compassionate community. In general, women are community builders, they're resourceful, and they allow people to shine. **We need to look within ourselves and see what we have that is unique and how we can contribute. There isn't any act of kindness that is too small. I think it will spiral outward. Those are the things that will change the world. It will shift it. I believe that we will see real changes when we replace our need to feel special or unique with the awareness that we are all a part of the big picture.**

Debbie

We
help
other
women
by
being
role
models.
I
think
that
doing
something
is
more
powerful
than
telling
other
people
what
to
do.

Cassandra

There are a lot of ugly things happening on the planet right now with environmental changes, pollutions, governments, and violence. But there's something else happening, which is a liberating of the Spirit. I think women are reaching out to each other in fearless honesty. We need to create a community of women to be real and to balance our society.

Women have been silent for so long out of fear and survival. When we were silent, that forced us to do some inner work.

The oppression that we went through deepened us. We were forced to look inside to keep our little glimmer of light, our Spirit, going. We're leading humanity and I think we're meant to. That's what I keep running into in my readings about the ancient teachers. That women are forced through some of our experiences to create inner strength, and through our cultural experience of being oppressed and silenced we had to find our inner strength. Things will get worse until it all breaks down, but the feminine influence will be ready to help the world.

Kristin

Women are less destructive. If women have more power, there would be less war, less pollution, less destruction. There just hasn't been balance. Women will balance things so earth can heal.

Sue

You have to work on it in yourself and then it spreads to the people around you. It becomes like a chain. Some people do huge things, but most of us do small things. What we do matters because of the ripple effect.

I think that if we don't honor female energy, we're doomed. I think the feminine is going to save us. And if we don't allow it to save us, we're gone. That's how important I think it is. I don't think we'll evolve unless we take the planet back.

Anne

When we talk it can be magical when we bounce ideas off each other. We need to stay connected to people, keep passing down what we're learning to make sure we stay open to what they have to say. We really thrive in groups. We have a right to wake up. I really think we should also stay connected with men and share the information.

Gretchen

Women need to be ready
for those who are going to come
needing **answers**, **guidance**,
nurturing, and **direction**.
We're midwifing this change
that's like a birth.

Lisa

I support other women through my conversations or interaction with them when the conversation turns toward their growth. When women start to wake up, you have to be really supportive, and acknowledge and validate them, and live by example.

The world can't keep going in the direction it's going. We need balance, the planet needs balance because it's heading toward destruction. We need female energy in every aspect of our universe.

We each have our own role, so it's learning what that role is, which is usually part of our purpose and where we find passion. Then we have to live that role.

Lynn

The best way is to continue to wake yourself up. You benefit others much more the more awake *you* are. Take any opportunity that comes to you to help others. Those opportunities are there all the time. Give love and compassion, share wisdom.

Heather

Women's greatest strength has been our ability to **communicate**. We actually talk to each other. We talk about feelings. We can be **open** and **loving** with each other. Our communion doesn't have to be through an activity. Our communion can be just because we really like each other and we talk. It's really **powerful**.

Women have the most important role in waking up the planet. There's something that we can offer that has been either shut down or diminished for so long. I don't know how it's going to unfold, how it will look. But the love that women can bring forth to help heal the planet will be so powerful.

LORI

We need strong, spiritual female
leaders to take us to that next level
and we don't have that yet. We
need more women like Oprah.

If we were the force, instead of the patriarchal force, there would be no wars. The wars are all perpetrated by men.

It starts at the ground level. At
the heart of our communities.

The key is we need to nurture the celebration of womanhood.

Women have been dismissed and they've
dismissed themselves. We should celebrate
ourselves.

Daphne

Each of us deep down knows what we're here to give. Ultimately, just giving what we're here to give wakes us all up. It's important for us to support each other emotionally and to hear the stories of other women who haven't followed the patriarchal path. Or who've tried to follow it and it hasn't fit for them.

Jan

The earth is dying and we are dying. Our spirits are dying because the water, earth and sky are filled with pollutants. They're killing us and the creatures around us. We heal the planet one breath at a time, one action at a time, one heartfelt connection at a time. And one small act of kindness at a time. Everything matters.

Both men and women embody female and male energies, yet male energy has been more outwardly "rewarded" in our society. It's about recognizing and, integrating these female/male energies within ourselves. Combining the softness with the power, the gentleness with the action. I feel that once we begin to accept responsibility for the state of our nations, our planet, we can create and catalyze change. It's already happening.

Sura

What a mess the world is in under the leadership of men. As we make inroads into positions of power it's very exciting to imagine the world with powerful, awake women. It will be such a wonderful, positive energy.

We are all connected. We are all born of the same stuff. We form the earth, the rock, the water, the people, and the plants. And we are all connected down to the atomic level. The positive energy that is coming from women waking up is automatically felt through the earth.

Renee

When women awaken to their own spirituality, they can honor the uniqueness that being a woman can bring to everyday life. When women are bound together in a common cause we can make the earth move. We can help the whole society function on a higher level spiritually because women are more connected to their own spirituality than men are.

Women are the channel between earth/nature and the spiritual realm. This female spirituality, when strong and organized, is amplified and is going to connect people to the planet. The more women who wake up—it's a pivotal part of how we save this planet from destruction.

Catherine

We have so many resources and abilities as women, and if we direct those toward other women, and they toward us, we can create an enormous amount of energy.

Joan

Patriarchy has brought the planet to where we are now. If women don't come together and use our energies to wake everyone up, we won't survive. We each play our part. We focus on who we are as spiritual beings and who we are as this particular soul who came onto the planet. We use all of our energy to find out who we are, what our part is, and we must do it now. Because we don't have much time. The planet is in big trouble, and this is the time.

$\mathcal{W}$hat began as a trickle of women awaking has now become a roaring river. I hope you, dear reader, will be inspired by these words to activate and strengthen your awakening process. The time is now, we are the ones we've been waiting for, women of the world wake up. We have a planet to save.

Resource Guide

Achterberg, Jeanne, *Woman as Healer: A Panoramic Sun of the Healing Activities of Women from Prehistoric Time to the Present.* Boston, Shambhala, 1991.

Ardagh, Arjona, *The Translucent Revolution: How People Just Like You Are Waking Up and Changing the World.* Novato, CA, New World Library, 2005.

Ban Breathnaeh, Sarah, *Something More: Excavating Your Authentic Self.* New York: Warner Books, 1998.

Beak, Sera, *The Red Book: A Deliciously Unorthodox Approach to Igniting Your Divine Spark.* San Francisco, Jossey-Bass, 2006.

Beck, Martha, *Finding Your Own North Star: Claiming the Life You Were Meant to Live.* New York, Three Rivers Press, 2001.

Bolen, Jean Shinoda, *Goddesses in Older Women: Archetypes in Women Over Fifty.* New York, HarperCollins, 2001.

Bolen, Jean Shinoda, *Crones Don't Whine: Concentrated Wisdom for Juicy Women.* San Francisco, Conari Press, 2003.

Bolen, Jean Shinoda, *Crossing to Avalon: A Woman's Midlife Quest for the Sacred Feminine.* New York, HarperCollins, 2004.

Bolen, Jean Shinoda, *Goddesses in Every Woman: Powerful Archetypes in Women's Lives.* New York, HarperCollins, 1985.

Bolen, Jean Shinoda, *The Millionth Circle: How to Change Ourselves and the World: The Essential Guide to Women's Circle.* San Francisco, Conari Press 2003.

Bolen, Jean Shinoda, *The Tao of Psychology: Synchronicity and the Self.* New York, HarperCollins, 1979.

Bolen, Jean Shinoda, *Urgent Message from Mother: Gather the Women, Save the World.* San Francisco, Condri Press, 2005.

Byron, Brown, *Soul Without Shame: A Guide to Liberating Yourself from the Judge Within.* Boston, Shambhala Publications, 1999.

Cameron, Julia, *The Right to Write: An Invitation and Initiation into the Writing Life.* New York, Penguin Putnam, 1998.

Carter-Scott, Cherie, *If Life is a Game, These are the Rules.* New York, Broadway Books, 1998.

Chopra, Deepak, *The Seven Spiritual Laws of Success: A Practical Guide to the Fulfillment of Your Dreams.* New World Library, 1993.

Clow, Barbara Hand, *The Mayan Code: Time Acceleration and Awakening the World Mind.* Rochester, VT: Bear and Company, 2007.

Cornell, Ann Weiser, *The Power of Focusing: A Practical Guide to Emotional Self-Healing*. New York, MJF Books, 1996.

Day, Laura, *Circle: How the Power of a Single Wish Can Change Your Life*. New York, Penguin Books, 2001.

DeSalvo, Louise, *Writing as a Way of Healing: How Telling Our Stories Transforms Our Lives*. Boston, Beacon Press, 1999.

Diamant, Anita, *The Red Tent*. New York, St. Martin's Press, 1997.

Fero, Patricia, *Mining for Diamonds: A Collection of Insights from Resilient Survivors of Adversity*. Rochester, WA, Gorham Printing, 2005.

Ford, Debbie, *The Right Questions: Ten Essential Questions to Guide You to an Extraordinary Life*. New York HarperCollins, 2003.

Gladwell, Malcolm, *The Tipping Point: How Little Things Can Make a Big Difference*. New York, Back Bay Books, 2000.

Hart, Hillary. *The Unknown She*.

Judith, Anodea, *Waking the Global Heart: Humanity's Rite of Passage from the Love of Power to the Power of Love*. Santa Rosa, CA Elite Books, 2006.

Louden, Jennifer, *The Woman's Retreat Book: A Guide to Restoring, Rediscovering, and Reawakening Your True Self – In a Moment, an Hour, a Day, or a Weekend*. San Francisco, Harper-Collins, 1997.

Marciniak, Barbara, *Family of Light*. Rochester, VT: Bean and Company, 1999.

Marciniak, Barbara, *Path of Empowerment: Pleigdian Wisdom for a World in Chaos: Creative Solutions for Changing Beliefs, Reclaiming Your Power, and Creating a World of Unlimited Possibilities*. Makawao, Maui, HI, Inner Ocean Publishing, Inc., 2004.

Markova, Dawna, *I Will Not Die an Unlived Life: Reclaiming Purpose and Passion*. Boston: Red Wheel, Weiser, 2000.

Matthews, Caitlin, *Psychic Shield: A Personal Handbook of Psychic Protection*. Berkeley, CA: Ulysses Press, 2006.

McBride, Karyl, *Will I Ever Be Good Enough? Healing the Daughters of Narcissistic Mother*s. New York, Free Press, 2008.

Mehdi, Sharon, *The Great Silent Grandmother Gathering: A Story for Anyone Who Thinks She Can't Save the World*. New York: Penguin Group, 2004.

Melchizedek, Drunvalo, *Serpent of Light: Beyond 2012: The Movement of the Earth's Kundalini and the Rise of the Female Light, 1949 to 2013*. San Francisco: Red Wheel/Weiser, 2008.

Nelson, Ruby, *The Door of Everything*. Marina del Rey, CA, Book Graphics, 1963.

Ni, Hua-Ching; Ni, Maoshing, *The Power of the Feminine: Using Feminine Energy to Heal the World's Spiritual Problems*. Los Angeles, Seven Star Communications, 2004.

Pert, Candace B., *Everything You Need to Know to Feel Go(o)d*. U.S. Hay House, 2006.

Pipher, Mary, *Writing to Change the World*. New York, Riverhead Books, 2006.

Pogacnik, Marko, *The Daughter of Gaia: Rebirth of the Divine Feminine*. Scotland, UK, Findhorn Press, 2001.

Reilly, Patricia Lynn, *A God Who Looks Like Me: Discovering a Woman-Affirming Spirituality*. Toronto, Ballentine Books, 1995.

Reilly, Patricia Lynn, *Imagine a Woman in Love with Herself: Embracing Your Wisdom and Wholeness*. Boston, Conari Press, 1999.

Richardson, Cheryl, *Life Makeovers: 52 Practical and Inspiring Ways to Improve Your Life One Week at a Time*. New York, Broadway Books, 2000.

Richardson, Cheryl, *Stand Up for Your Life: A Practical Step-by-Step Plan to Build Inner Confidence and Personal Power*. New York, Free Press, 2002.

Richardson, Cheryl, *The Unmistakable Touch of Grace: How to Recognize and Respond to the Spiritual Signposts in Your Life*. New York, Free Press, 2005.

Shafer, Carol, *Grandmothers Counsel the World*. Trumpeter Books, 2006.

Small, Jacqueline. *Becoming a Practical Mystic*. Harper Collins, NY, 1995.

Steinem, Gloria, *Revolution from Within: A Book of Self Esteem*. Canada, Little, Brown & Co., 1992.

Stone, Hal & Sidra, *Embracing Ourselves: The Voice Dialogue Manual*. Mill Valley, CA, Nataraj Publishing, 1989.

Taylor, Robert, *Into the Mystical: Ancient Wisdom for Our Troubled Times*. Ananta Publishing, 2008.

Telynoro, Jhehah, *Avalon Within: Inner Sovereignty and personal Transformation through the Avalonian Mysteries*. Book Surge, 2004.

Thoele, Sue, Patton, *A Woman's Book of Soul: Meditations for Courage, Confidence, and Spirit*. New York, MJF Books, 1998.

Tolle, Echart, *A New Earth: Awakening to Your Life's Purpose*. New York, Penguin Group, 2005.

Tolle, Echart, *The Power of Now: A Guide to Spiritual Enlightenment*. Novato, CA, 1999.

Villoldo, Alberto, *The Four Insights: Wisdom, Power, and Grace of the Earthkeepers*. U.S. Hay House, 2006.

Weiss, Brain L., M.D. *Many Lives, Many Masters: The True Story of a Prominent Psychiatrist, His Young Patient, and the Past Life Therapy That Changed Both Their Lives*. New York, Fireside, 1988.

Williamson, Marianne, *Everyday Grace: Having Hope, Finding Forgiveness, and Making Miracles*. New York, Riverhead Books, 2002.

Williamson, Marianne, *Illuminata: Thoughts, Prayers, Rites of Passage*. New York, Random House, 1994.

Williamson, Marianne, *The Age of Miracles, Embracing the New Midlife*. Hay House, Inc., 2008.

Williamson, Marianne, *The Gift of Change: Spiritual Guidance for a Radically New Life*. New York, HarperCollins, 2004.

Wolinsky, Stephen, *Trances People Live: Healing Approaches in Quantum Psychology*. Las Vegas, Bramble Co., 1991.

Zapf, Kimmie Rose, *Wake Up Your Intuition: A Clairvoyant Reveals the Psychic Process*. Kill Devil Hills, NC, Transpersonal Publishing, 2008.

Zukav, Gary and Francis, Linda, *The Heart of the Soul: Emotional Awareness*. New York, Simon and Schuster, 2001.

Websites

GathertheWomen.org
Wiseearth.org
World Changing.com
Carbon Fund.org
Waking the Global Heart.com
ImagineAWoman.com
Hay House.com
Oprah.com
Marianne Williamson.com
Heartmath.com
Standing Women.org
Women for Women International.org
Peace X Peace.org
Pachamama Alliance.org
Women at Heart.com

About the Author

PATRICIA FERO sees helping women wake up as her "Divine Assignment." She facilitates workshops, retreats, and does public speaking on this topic. she also specializes in resiliency based on her book *Mining for Diamonds*. A psychotherapist, who works with her therapy dog, Daisy, Patricia lives in Ann Arbor, Michigan.

Contact Information

www.PatriciaFero.com | e-mail: pat_fero@yahoo.com | Phone: 734-973-0817 | 3830 Packard St, Ste 250, Ann Arbor, MI 48108